Story
Dictation
A Guide for Early Childhood Professionals

Story
Dictation

A Guide for Early Childhood Professionals

Ann *Gadzikowski*

Redleaf Press
www.redleafpress.org
800-423-8309

Published by Redleaf Press
10 Yorkton Court
St. Paul, MN 55117
www.redleafpress.org

First edition 2007
Cover design by Amy Kirkpatrick
Cover photograph by Steve Wewerka
Interior typeset in Adobe Garamond Pro and designed by Dorie McClelland
Interior graphics by Amy Kirkpatrick
Photographs by the author and Steve Wewerka
Printed in the United States of America
14 13 12 11 10 09 08 07   1 2 3 4 5 6 7 8

The epigraph on p. 7 is from "Why We Tell Stories" in *The Need to Hold Still: Poems by Lisel Mueller.* © 1980 by Lisel Mueller. Reprinted with permission from Louisiana State University Press.

Personal communication on p. 64 reprinted with permission from Gillian McNamee.
Personal communication on p. 149 reprinted with permission from Esme Raji Codell.

Library of Congress Cataloging-in-Publication Data
Gadzikowski, Ann.
  Story dictation : a guide for early childhood professionals / Ann Gadzikowski.
     p. cm.
  Includes bibliographical references.
  ISBN 978-1-933653-28-0 (alk. paper)
  1. Storytelling. 2. Storytelling ability in children. 3. Language arts (Early childhood)
4. Early childhood educators—Training of. I. Title.
  LB1042.G23 2007
  372.67'7—dc22

                         2007020598

Printed on 30 percent post–consumer waste paper

To my friends and mentors
at the Erikson Institute,
past and present

Story Dictation

Foreword

Wherever there are children, stories are being invented. Plots and characters are stepping onto imaginary stages at an amazing rate. Listening to the voices of the young in Ann Gadzikowski's sensitive and persuasive study of story dictation and its natural partners of drama and play, we are again reminded of our creative beginnings.

"Once upon a time a wind came blowing and blowing. Superbird came because he was in danger," says Keisha. And, indeed, children's dreamlike imagery does seem to blow across the landscape. "Once there was a boy named Nick and he met an alien. And the alien had six eyes," Jack dictates, while Kathy tells us, "The princess rode on a unicorn to the castle." But for little Nathan, the wind blows into his own kitchen. "My papa is funny. I runs around and laughs a lot."

What are we to do with this never-ending supply of stories? Children, of course, never ask such a question, for to them fantasy is the breath of life. But for us grown-ups, who need reassurance that there's a road map for our journey, Ms. Gadzikowski provides reliable guideposts we can follow in our quest for teachable moments and learning opportunities.

She also makes it clear that it is the children themselves who continually nurture the narrative flow that binds us together in a community that is "all ears." Her respect for children and her understanding of the child-teacher relationship enable us to explore story dictation as the conduit through which the uniqueness of each child's contribution can be recognized and valued.

Ms. Gadzikowski presents a careful analysis of the process, while at the same time preserving its magical component. Armed with practical suggestions and scenarios, the reader learns to become Listener, Scribe, and Stage Director at the moment of creation. We all have our roles to play, but the leading actors clearly are the children themselves. It is their stories that inspire and instruct Ms. Gadzikowski, and she passes the lessons along to us with clarity and insight.

—Vivian Gussin Paley

Acknowledgments

I am very grateful to all the children who shared their stories with me, most recently the children of Group C at the Child Care Center of Evanston. Many thanks to Group C teachers, Bettye Cohns and Belinda Bester, for welcoming me into their classroom.

Special thanks to Richard and Alexa for their patience, encouragement, and support.

Many thanks to the following educators, families, and programs, who contributed information and stories for this book: Debbie Boileve, Eryn Brissette-Jones, Meredith Chambers, Janet Kelly, Linda Li, Delores Malone, Gillian McNamee, Larissa Mulholland, Vivian Gussin Paley, Heather Refroe, Laurie Sahn, Felicia Stratten, Natalie Wainwright, Olga Winbush, Dave Winter, and Kathy Young; the Frankfurter family, the Hoffman Kimball family, the Knoblock family, the Laughlin Ferry family, the Morrison Silverstein family, the Ohman-Rodriguez family, the Thompson family, and the Tseng family; Aunt Martha's Riverdale Head Start, Beth Emet Preschool, Cherry Preschool, Chinese American Service League Child Development Center, Evanston Day Nursery, McGaw YMCA Child Care Center, Reba Early Learning Center, School for Little Children, and Total Child Center.

All Ears: Listening to the Stories of Young Children

Back in the old days, when children weren't expected to learn how to read until they entered first grade, I attended a red brick elementary school in suburban Chicago. My first-grade teacher, Mrs. Jackson, taught us to read using a set of primers very similar to the classic Dick and Jane books, except that the main characters in our primers were a girl named Ann and a boy named Bob. Since my own name is Ann and a boy in my class was named Bob, the primers made perfect sense to me. ("Come, Ann. Come and see. Look at Bob.") Never mind that the real Bob was a sullen boy who rarely spoke to me. I learned to read quickly and enthusiastically. How lucky I was to be the star of the first stories I ever read.

Now, as an adult, I can imagine that the other children in my class, though possessed of perfectly fine names like Maya, Anton, and Suzette, probably did not feel the thrill I felt when we read our primers. And realizing that has led me to wonder whether early childhood education might not be transformed if all children had the chance to star in the first stories they encountered in school.

My fascination with children's story dictation began with this idea that children learning to read will be most interested in stories that have a direct connection to their own lives. We know that children (and adults, too, for that matter) will pay attention to things that are important to them. So a child whose mother is a waitress is probably going to be very interested in a story that takes place in a restaurant. And a child living in Minnesota is probably going to be more interested in a sledding story than a child in Florida would be. If we want children to pay attention to the written word, we have to offer them stories that are so fascinating and meaningful they can't possibly turn away. And we needn't look far. The children will tell us these stories themselves.

> Once upon a time a long long long time ago when Alex was here he was
> so silly I laughed so hard I had to go to the potty.
> *Maddie, age 4*

The term *story dictation* describes what happens when a child tells a story (or offers a description of an event or a person, which is called a narrative) and an adult or an older child writes down the child's words, exactly as the child has spoken them.

Story dictation is already practiced in many early childhood settings. The teacher and the child sit side by side at a low table. The teacher's pencil is poised above the blank page, like a diver about to plunge into the water. The teacher turns her face to the child, and their eyes meet. As the child begins to speak, the teacher's hand begins to move across the page. The day's story dictation has begun.

> I wake up by myself. My mommy give my sister and me milk. Everyone
> put socks on. My mommy put her shoes on. My sister put her shoes on and
> I put my shoes on too. My mommy drive me to school. I eat breakfast at
> school and I brush my teeth. I tell story. Miss Linda write the story. The end.
> *Peter, age 4*

Story dictation is a valuable part of any early childhood setting because it fosters children's language, literacy, and social and emotional development. The stories it generates can also be included in a child's portfolio and used as an assessment tool. It is also an activity that helps to develop a lifelong love of stories and books. But what is perhaps most important, the very act of dictating a story gives a child the gift of the caregiver's full attention, helping to build a secure and trusting relationship between caregiver and child.

Most early literacy activities take place in groups. Picture books are read aloud to groups of children during story time. Groups of preschool children are encouraged to play games with sentence strips or alphabet cards. But during story dictation, children enjoy the one-on-one attention of a caregiver. It only makes sense that a child is more likely to express himself creatively and try out new words and ideas when a caregiver listens attentively to what he says and shows her respect for his words by carefully writing them down.

Doing story dictation is a little like trying to save the rain forest; everyone agrees it's a good idea, but no one is completely sure of how to go about it.

Having practiced and observed a variety of approaches to story dictation during my many years as a teacher and director of early childhood programs, it concerns me that many early childhood professionals are reluctant to try story dictation because they're afraid of not doing it correctly. For example, teachers often think that if they don't do story dictation every day, they shouldn't do it at all. And many teachers believe that stories should be dictated only if they're going to be dramatized or acted out in a group. But I believe that something is always better than nothing.

This book grew out of my desire to reassure teachers and caregivers that there is no wrong way to do story dictation. The only requirement is a willingness to try—to show up with paper and pencil, ready to listen and write. During my research for the book, as I talked with dozens of teachers and collected hundreds of story samples, one constant soon emerged: although no two teachers approached story dictation in quite the same way, every child had benefited from the opportunity to tell her story and be heard.

This book is intended for early childhood providers at all levels of education and experience. If you've never tried story dictation, this book will help you take those first steps. If you've tried it but aren't sure you're doing it "right," this book will show you that—contrary to anything you may have heard—there truly is no wrong way to do story dictation. And if you're already doing story dictation regularly and have witnessed firsthand the amazing results, this book will help you look even deeper into the magic of children's stories.

The three parts of this book answer the "why," "how," and "what" questions about story dictation. Part I addresses why people tell stories, why we do story dictation with young children, and how the developmental stages young children go through affect the way they tell stories. Part II explains how to create a time and space for story dictation in an early childhood classroom or a family child care home. It also offers a variety of strategies for building on the stories, such as acting them out, sharing them with families, and using them for assessment and curriculum development. Finally, by examining common themes and patterns, Part III of this book looks at what children's stories mean.

If you're ready to take that first simple step, pick up your pencil and say, "How does your story begin?"

PART 1

Why We Do Story Dictation

Before doing story dictation in an early childhood setting, you might find it helpful to look at why stories matter in the lives of young children. Part I describes the important functions stories serve in all our lives, especially those of children and families, by looking at the roles of culture and identity in storytelling, the many ways stories help us build relationships, and what children learn from the storytelling process.

1 Why We Tell Stories

Because we used to have leaves
and on damp days
our muscles feel a tug,
painful now, from when roots
pulled us into the ground

and because our children believe
they can fly, an instinct retained
from when the bones in our arms
were shaped like zithers and broke
neatly under their feathers

and because before we had lungs
we knew how far it was to the bottom
as we floated open-eyed
like painted scarves through the scenery
of dreams, and because we awakened

and learned to speak

—Lisel Mueller, from "Why We Tell Stories"

Lisel Mueller's poem beautifully describes the desire to create stories, a desire that awakens in children as soon as they speak their first words. This chapter examines our human desire to share stories with others.

Think about a story you enjoyed when you were a child. Perhaps it was a fairytale in a book, or a story that never was captured on paper but was told aloud by members of your family. Think about why that story was important to you. How did hearing the story make you feel? Perhaps the story taught you something important about yourself or about your world. Or maybe it was important simply because the person who shared it with you was someone you dearly loved.

Stories and storytelling help us build relationships, share culture, explore our identities, and in some cases, reconcile difficult emotions. We explore each of these issues in the sections that follow.

Making Connections

There are many good reasons for teaching children to read and write. We know, of course, that when they grow up, they'll need to read and write in order to function in the world, to handle practical tasks like cooking, driving, and getting a job. More immediately, children need to read and write in order to do well in school. In fact, when teachers and parents discuss children's reading and writing, the focus usually is on success in school. In particular, there's a great deal of urgency around learning to read, a milestone we encourage children to pass as quickly as possible, as if it's a race to a finish line.

But the most important reason is so fundamental, so obvious, that like the air we breathe, we sometimes forget it's there: we read and write to communicate with other human beings, to connect with each other. When they have the experience of sharing their stories with others, even very young children can begin to understand the connecting power of reading and writing. And it is within the context of their own families that they first experience that power.

Families and Culture

Family life is full of stories. A child may hear her father tell her mother how he misplaced his car keys and then, after looking everywhere in the house, finally found them in his own pocket. Or the child may listen to her mother tell a friend over the phone what happened to a character on a television show the previous night. Then there are the stories told directly to the child at bedtime, in the car, or at the dinner table. Some stories are read aloud from books. Stories are created spontaneously. Funny stories and stories about important family events are told and retold. Gathering in all such experiences, children learn how stories can be used to build connections, transfer information, and gain support.

> When I wake up I watch television in Granny's room. My mommy takes
> me to Warren's and I get my hair cut. And then my mommy takes me to my
> other grandma's house. My mommy tells me stories about alligators.
> *Terrance, age 4*

Stories help create a warm bond between parent and child. Children often are particularly interested in stories about when their parents were children. Looking at family photo albums together can inspire this kind of storytelling. Parents and other family members may also use stories to teach important lessons. "You must never run out into the street. When I was little I ran into the street chasing a ball, and I almost got hit by a car." These kinds of stories give children a sense of their family history and culture.

Stories parents read aloud to children have a positive influence on them.

Children learn to tell their own stories by imitating the stories that are told to them. Although children are eventually very much influenced by the stories that are read to them, such as fairytales, or by the stories they see on television, they model their first stories on those that are told to them by their families.

Stories and Identity

It is no surprise, then, that when children have the opportunity to tell their own stories, the most popular subject is their own family. Such stories help children define themselves within the context of their family. Often a young child's first attempt at telling a story is simply a list of the people in her family.

> My mommy and my daddy and my baby sister Janice Jordan Mariah.
> *Sadie, age 3*

> My mommy and Mimi and my daddy and my brother and Caroline and me.
> *Annie, age 3*

Stories such as these show how a child's sense of self is connected to and defined by his own family. In the following story a child describes her life in the context of events shared with her mother, her brother, and her sister.

> Me and my mommy picked out berries. And we picked out apples. And we ate them. And my mommy take me to basketball and we watch my brother play basketball. And me and my baby sister take baths together and we play in the bathtub.
> *Julissa, age 4*

Children's author Julius Lester has said that stories "illuminate where we've come from, who we are, and where we might be going." In the lives of young children, both the stories they hear and the stories they tell help them construct their identity, their sense of self, and their understanding of where they belong in the context of their family.

Many of the stories children tell us often are like mirrors reflecting the children's identities back to them.

> I love my mommy. And I play with my doggy and my mommy. And I play everything! And I do everything. And I play and I play with my mommy.
> *Daniel, age 3*

But stories do more than simply reflect what's already there. The process of telling the story also serves the important function of allowing children to actively construct an identity, to place pieces of a puzzle into empty spaces. Through storytelling, children actively create an internal image of who they are. Anyone who's ever kept a diary or journal will tell you that the process of naming experiences and feelings often creates new understanding. You may have had the experience of telling a friend about something and suddenly discovering that the conversation has allowed you to see things in a new light. A sense of recognition arises when we name our experiences.

As Susan Engel wrote in her book *The Stories Children Tell,* "Every story a child tells, acts out through play, or writes contributes to a self-portrait—a portrait that he can look at, refer to, think about, and change, a portrait others can use to develop an understanding of the storyteller" (1999, p. 1).

The Healing Power of Stories

Besides the power to entertain, to amuse, and to teach, stories also have the power to comfort and to heal. In the field of psychology, the therapeutic use of stories is sometimes referred to as bibliotherapy (Pardeck and Pardeck 1993). This kind of therapy is based on the idea that when we tell stories, we express our ideas and feelings. Likewise, when we listen to or read stories we identify with the feelings and experiences described in them. Sharing stories allows both teller and listener to release emotional tension and to gain insight about themselves and others.

Luckily, enjoying the healing power of stories doesn't require the help of a therapist. This kind of healing takes place in ordinary settings, such as on a sunny rug in a preschool classroom. The telling and sharing of stories can promote healing for children who have experienced trauma and anxiety. This process also provides opportunities for social growth and emotional development that can benefit any child.

Early childhood professionals often talk about the importance of caring for "the whole child." By this we mean that all areas of child development—physical, emotional, social, cognitive, language development, and so on—are closely related. Story dictation offers significant support to a child's development in all these domains, but it especially addresses the important links between language development and emotional development. Both for typically developing children and for children with special needs, the sharing of experiences diminishes feelings of isolation and allows children to feel empowered (Koplow 1996, p. 8). But we don't need research data to tell us how good it feels when someone really listens to us: the experience of speaking and being heard is valued everywhere.

> The bear went outside to pick strawberries. He saw a skunk and the skunk came up to him and said, "Are you a skunk too?" The bear said, "No, I am not a skunk. I live in a cave." "Oh, I live in a cave too," the skunk said. "We're friends and we like to play together." The end.
>
> *Ryan, age 4*

TEACHING TIPS

- Be a storytelling role model for the children in your care. Tell the children informal, brief stories from your own experiences. "Did I ever tell you about the time I forgot to put the lid on the playdough? When I took out the playdough container the next morning, what do you think I found? A lump of playdough that was as hard as a rock!"

- Encourage parents to tell their own stories to their children. In your school newsletter, include "story starter" ideas like the following one for parents to try at home. "Tell your child about one of your own childhood experiences, such as your first day of school, or a good time you had playing with a favorite friend, or a fun family gathering."

- Post family photos in your classroom at children's eye level. Prompt children to express their ideas by saying, "Tell me about your family," or "Tell me about this picture." Then label the photos with the children's words or sentences.

2

Why We Do Story Dictation

When I was a preschool teacher, I worked with children who were separated from their families for nine or ten hours each workday. Knowing how important it was that the children feel safe and secure at school, I tried in several ways to demonstrate that they could trust me. I developed predictable routines so they knew what would happen during each part of the day. I made sure that they observed positive interactions between me and their parents. And, perhaps most important, I built trust by simply listening to them.

This chapter describes how listening to children during the story dictation process helps to build trusting relationships between caregivers and children. It also deals with how story dictation gives the provider important information about individual children, supports children's social and emotional development by promoting friendships between children, and enables an early childhood curriculum to meet a broad range of learning standards.

Story Dictation Builds Relationships

Story dictation is a social interaction, an invitation from the adult and a response from the child, that contributes to the development of a trusting relationship between them. The teacher gives the child the gift of her full attention, which invites the child to open up and respond. As children participate in story dictation regularly over a period of time, they gradually come to feel more and more at ease in expressing their feelings and ideas. Story dictation is an especially valuable practice in working with vulnerable children who have difficulty using language or building trusting relationships with their caregivers.

During the story dictation process, the teacher and child create something special: a story on paper. With an encouraging manner and open-ended questions, the teacher leads the child through the creation of the story. The deepening of their relationship as they work together to produce the child's finished story can be very satisfying to both of them. When I was teaching, the primary reason I did story dictation was to strengthen my relationships with the children in my care.

Story Dictation Helps You Learn about the Children in Your Care

In this book, I use the word *assessment* to describe the ways teachers and child care providers get to know the children in their care. Each time we learn a bit more about a child, we become better teachers. It is a natural, intuitive process. True assessment is more about understanding than about measuring. It is also part of building strong relationships.

Assessment can be informal or formal. Getting to know a child through casual conversation, chance observation, and storytelling is informal assessment. More formal assessment practices include documenting children's growth and progress through the development of child portfolios. Either kind of assessment can be a source of important information for teachers.

Listening to the stories a child tells is one of the best ways to get to know that child. His stories offer a unique opportunity to understand what makes him tick, how he thinks, and what he knows about the world. Through children's stories we can find out what interests them, what they're wondering about, what frightens them, and what makes them feel passionate.

The Brave of the Girls
Mary, Lindsey, and Mikayla hopped on their surfboards at the beach. They saw a boat. "The boat is sinking!" said Mary. They rescued the pirates from the sinking ship. They hopped on a giant surfboard and went slashing through the sea. They went to a hotel. Mary worked on her book about boats in the middle of the night. The pirates yawned and fell asleep. The next day the pirates told the girls where their mom was. They smiled and ran to their mom.
Heidi, age 5

By reading "The Brave of the Girls," we know that Heidi has a vivid imagination and a good vocabulary. We can also make some educated guesses about her interests and personality. Heidi's choice to tell a story about a group of brave girls tells us that she probably values her friendships with other girls and enjoys thinking of girls as active and powerful. We can also guess that Heidi loves and values books, because in her story her character Mary is writing her own book.

Informal assessment takes place every time a teacher or caregiver listens to a child's story. We can even liken it to what happens when you make a new friend. You probably want to find out what your friend likes to do for fun or what your friend likes to eat. You want to know what makes your friend laugh. You may want to know what your friend's family is like. You probably want to know what fears or worries your friend has. You want to know what your friend's interests are and what hopes for the future your friend has.

In the context of a story, a child will share this kind of information with you naturally. Of course, since children freely mix truth with fiction, if a child says in her story that she has a new baby brother, that may or may not be true. Some outside verification of facts may be necessary. But even a make-believe story reveals a child's feelings and interests. If we listen with a flexible ear, noting most the emotions and passions in a story, we will learn a great deal indeed.

> Once upon a time there was a snowman. He rescued a penguin from a bad
> pig. The bad pig was a vampire pig. He was a bad one. The snowman had a
> play date with the penguin. The penguin said, "Okay. Can we play?"
> *Adam, age 4*

This story reveals, for example, that Adam may be especially interested in learning about penguins and engaging in pretend play related to penguins, snow, and cold places. The ending of his story also suggests that Adam has some understanding of how to make friends and initiate play with other children.

Unlike many formal assessment tools, such as checklists that require eliciting specific responses from a child ("Can you tell me the name of this letter?"), children's dictated stories are a natural and authentic source of information. This makes story dictation an extremely valuable practice. Like a good talk with a friend, a child's story may reveal emotions and interests that might never be touched upon through direct questioning. When these connections are made, our teaching improves naturally, because we are better able to tailor our teaching to the needs and interests of the children. By assessing (or, in other words, by understanding) children in this way, our relationships become stronger and we become better teachers.

Story Dictation Fosters Friendships

The positive influence of the story dictation process becomes even broader when children share their stories with each other. Of the many ways teachers and child care providers can facilitate friendships and partnerships between children, story dictation is one of the most powerful. We can use it to bring children together, to teach them to listen to each other, and to show them what they have in common.

We can foster friendships during the story dictation process by modeling for children what respectful listening is. Since story dictation usually takes place in the middle of a bustling room, other children are often observing and listening while a teacher is writing down a child's words. The teacher shows that she is listening to that child by tilting her head toward the storyteller, by moving her gaze from the page to the speaker's face, and by providing encouragement through occasionally nodding her head or asking questions, such as "Yes, now what comes next?" The teacher also models respectful listening by responding to the inevitable interruptions with statements, such as "I'll help you in a minute. Right now I'm listening to Marina's story."

This kind of respectful listening on the part of the teacher or child care provider encourages the other children to listen and interact in respectful ways. For example, if story dictation takes place at a writing table during free play, there usually will be other children at the table besides the child who is dictating a story. The other children may be writing and drawing, or waiting for a turn to tell their own stories. Since such an arrangement invites listening, conversation, and collaboration, the children may spontaneously respond to each other's stories as they are being told and even offer ideas and suggestions. Doing so is evidence that the children are listening carefully to each other. The teacher or provider can facilitate partnerships and friendships at the writing table by keeping interruptions brief and helping to clarify the suggestions that are made. Although some timid children may feel overwhelmed by suggestions from other children, most will welcome the positive attention and interesting ideas they get while they're in the role of storyteller.

In her book *The Boy Who Would Be a Helicopter: The Uses of Storytelling in the Classroom*, Vivian Gussin Paley writes that the best thing she did as a teacher was to use the children's dictated stories to draw "invisible lines" between the children, fostering connections that enriched the classroom community (1990, p. xi). Children learn what they have in common when they listen to each other's stories, both when the stories are told and later, when they're read aloud to the class. The expectation that connections will be made can be stated explicitly as the teacher or child care provider introduces a story. "Let's listen to Nathan's story. I'm wondering if anything like this has ever happened to any of you."

> My papa is funny. I runs around and laughs around. My momma and my papa eat supper with me. I always sleep backwards on my bed. My turtle and my bunny are snuggling together. My bunny is sometimes by herself in the washer.
>
> *Nathan, age 3*

Any child who has watched a cherished stuffed animal churn in a washing machine can strongly identify with the last line of this story. When this story is read aloud to Nathan's class, children are likely to experience a sense of recognition and may spontaneously comment, "That happened to me too!" Or the teacher can invite children to discuss these connections by asking, "Does Nathan's story remind you of anything that has happened in your life?" When such connections are made, children are likely to find that they have much in common.

Dictated stories also can be used to make connections between children during play. For example, one day Shaun, who enjoys telling stories about aliens, was having trouble finding someone to play with on the playground. Shaun's teacher helped him find a playmate by saying to another child, "Remember that story Shaun told about the aliens? Would you like to play aliens with Shaun? The climber could be your spaceship."

A community is a place where connections are made. During the story dictation process, connections are made through listening, observing, and learning about and appreciating one another. Once children experience connections with others through their stories, not only do the stories they tell become even more interesting, but the classroom or child care setting becomes more cooperative and friendly, and the opportunities for learning become even richer.

Story Dictation Helps Meet Learning Standards

Current public policies put pressure on early childhood educators to achieve more and to achieve it sooner. A recent study coordinated by the High/Scope Educational Research Foundation found that for many teachers, the struggle to align their teaching practices with specific learning standards often resulted in their engaging in ineffective teaching practices, such as whole-group direct instruction (Jacobson 2006). Story dictation offers an alternative: a child-centered, imaginative, and open-ended curriculum activity that yields tangible, measurable results and helps address a wide range of early learning standards (see chapter 8).

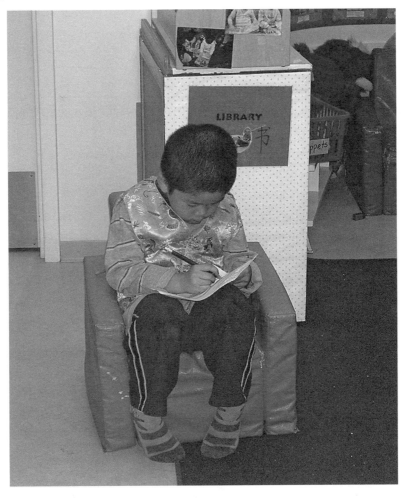

Story dictation inspires children to experiment with words and writing.

The richest and most obvious opportunities for learning through story dictation are in the area of language and literacy development. The story dictation process encourages children to express their ideas in words, expand their vocabularies, and speak in sentences. Creating and retelling stories helps children develop their understanding of literary conventions, such as story structure (beginning, middle, and end) and dialogue. Creating written stories, with an adult managing the writing process, also helps children learn concepts about print, such as letter recognition, phonics, and a beginning sight vocabulary.

Expanding language and literacy skills is an essential part of children's cognitive development. Creating stories stretches children's imaginations, which, in turn, helps to develop abstract thinking. Storytelling also helps children develop problem-solving skills, understanding of cause and effect relationships, and ability to compare and contrast. In addition, children's stories often provide opportunities for demonstrating and expanding upon children's understanding of math and science concepts. For example, the stories may include numbers and quantities or explore physical properties.

As this chapter has explained, story dictation helps build relationships, which promotes children's social-emotional development. Creating stories also can help children understand and describe both their own emotions and the emotions of others, and it can help children develop confidence by building a strong sense of self.

If practicing emerging writing skills is part of the process, story dictation can contribute to children's small-motor development, and large-motor development might be supported if children act out their stories as a group, using their bodies to represent characters and events in their stories.

TEACHING TIPS

- Practice paying close attention to how much time you spend listening each day. You'll probably notice how frequently, for the sake of group management, you must interrupt children's conversations. Practice listening to children more attentively. At the snack table, on the playground, or at the art table, make a conscious effort to listen rather than talk.

- Use children's dictated stories to identify common interests between children and to then encourage friendships. When helping young children make friends, try pairing children who have similar interests but not necessarily similar personalities. Remember that because sometimes opposites do attract, sometimes quiet, timid children enjoy the company of more gregarious companions.

- Keep in mind that story dictation can be a good way to help a new child feel welcome. Encourage a new child to sit next to you as you take dictation from other children. She will feel more secure sitting close to you, and she'll also learn how to tell stories by listening to and observing the other children. Soon she'll also be telling her own stories.

- In both individual and class portfolios, use dictated stories to document children's learning.

3

How Young Children Tell Stories

A day of teaching young children can be full of surprises. Recently I had the experience of sitting down with a three-year-old child to help her dictate her first story. When she opened her mouth to speak, she said, "El em en oh pee." Not sure that I understood what she said, I asked her to repeat it. "El em en oh pee!" It took me another moment to realize that she was dictating the names of letters of the alphabet. I wrote down the letters L-M-N-O-P and asked, "What comes next in your story?" She replied, "Em es tee el aye em en pee." I wrote M-S-T-L-A-M-N-P. I had to resist the temptation to say this wasn't a story, it was just letters. When she'd finished dictating, I read the letters back to her, and her bright smile told me she was completely satisfied with her story. Setting aside my disappointment that her story didn't have characters, action, or even words, I recognized that this child was fascinated with letters and enjoyed seeing the letters she dictated appear on the page. I realized that this unconventional story had provided a rich and exciting literacy experience for this particular child.

This interaction reminded me that the stories dictated by young children often do not follow the patterns of conventional adult storytelling. Every child is unique, and that makes the possibilities for creative storytelling endless. But it's also true that children's stories tend to follow some broad and predictable patterns that are related to child development.

Knowing what the developmentally appropriate expectations for children's storytelling are can be especially helpful if you are new to story dictation. Understanding storytelling patterns helps us teachers and caregivers respond with acceptance and encouragement when children first attempt story dictation. When we can predict what skills are likely to unfold next, we are better able to guide the development of children's storytelling skills. We can also better assess children's dictated stories when we understand how stories relate to children's overall development.

First Stories

Children can be encouraged to begin dictating stories as soon as they're able to speak in sentences. This usually occurs around the time a child turns three years old. Children's earliest spoken sentences usually are very short, just three or four words, such as, "Mommy drives the car" or "Soup is hot," and their earliest stories are also very short.

First attempts at telling a story, regardless of the age at which a child begins dictating stories, may consist of only one or two words.

> Mommy.
> *Kayla, age 3*

When doing story dictation with young preschoolers, keep in mind that the words children dictate will be more like brief comments, descriptions, or narratives than actual stories.

> Fast car. Zoom.
> *Ricky, age 3*

Some stories may be in the form of a list rather than a sentence.

> An alligator, a fish, and a shark.
> *Roy, age 3*

Even four- and five-year-olds may dictate only a handful of words at a time if the story dictation process is new to them. But once a child has had some experience with story dictation, his dictated sentences will begin to match, and in some cases surpass, the sentences he uses in everyday conversation.

> I saw Andrew at Chuck E. Cheese. I was there with my cousin.
> *Darren, age 3*

And just as children's sentences become more complex as children develop, so do their story lines.

> Me and my mom were catching my cat when she ran away. And then me and
> Daniel ran after my mom. We caught my cat. Then we brought her home.
> *Patricia, age 4*

As young children get older, they develop the cognitive ability to think not only about the present moment but also about future events. It is at this stage that children may begin telling stories that express wishes or hopes for the future.

> I really want a dog. I would play with it.
> *Jake, age 4*

This development goes hand in hand with children's growing comprehension of abstraction, and together these abilities have a great influence on children's pretend play and storytelling.

Stories and Pretend Play

Stories, like play, are a natural product of childhood. Children will create stories naturally and spontaneously when we give them the time, space, and encouragement to do so. And like play, story dictation helps children grow and develop, express themselves, try out new roles and ideas, and learn new skills.

Sometimes there is no clear boundary between stories and play. Children's pretend play often is inspired by the stories that have been read or told to them or by stories they've told themselves. Likewise, many of the most imaginative stories children tell are extensions of their own pretend play.

In many ways, the progression of children's stories from simple to sophisticated parallels the way children's pretend play develops as they grow and mature.

A child's first attempts at pretend play, which usually occur around the time a child turns two, will be quite simple. A bowl becomes a hat. A shoe becomes a boat. Gradually the child develops the ability to pretend in social play with other children. A three-year-old's pretend scenarios are usually based on familiar reality—"You be the mommy and I'll be the baby." Later, at age four or five, the child will begin to incorporate more fantastical characters and concepts, such as magic and monsters, into her pretend play.

As with pretend play, the topic of a child's first story often is something familiar, such as family, friends, or school.

> I went to Peter and Henry's house and I came back. I stayed home and
> Peter and Henry came to our house.
> *Luke, age 4*

Older preschoolers and kindergarteners, whose cognitive development has enabled them to think more abstractly, will also tell imaginative stories of magic and adventure.

> The dragon hid jewels in a cave. The knight smelled the jewels. He put a
> spell on the dragon. He took the gold and rubies and brought them back to
> the castle.
> *Charles, age 5*

We can expect the stories a child dictates to become more complex over time. With repeated practice, the child will gain more confidence as a storyteller, develop a larger vocabulary, and begin to think more abstractly. Children around the age of five and older have the ability, and often the desire, to tell longer, more imaginative stories.

> There were some superheroes and some dinosaurs too. The dinosaurs ate
> the superheroes. The superheroes raced up inside the dinosaurs and tried
> to punch their teeth out so they could get out, and punched only one out.
> Laser Beam Guy used his laser and shot two teeth out. They had to shoot
> all their teeth out. There were five dinosaurs and five superheroes, one
> inside each dinosaur. And there's a guy named Flame-On and he shoots
> fire and he shot three teeth out! This one's Lemon Guy and he shoots tons
> of lemons. Boom! Boom! Boom! Boom! He shot out four teeth.
>
> Now there was another girl named Leaf Girl. She shoots leaves. Puchoo!
> Puchoo! Puchoo! Puchoo! Puchoo! Five! And then there was Hydro Man.
> He's mostly made of water, or he can turn into a boy but he likes to be water.
> He shoots six teeth. He shoots the farthest—thirty-three feet! The superheroes

"Maybe we should bring the ruby to the
King and queen in the dark cave."
So they traveled and traveled on a
big boat until they reached land. They
saw a scary dark cave with two
chairs in it. A king and queen were
sitting in them. So the two unicorns
handed the ruby to the king and queen.
The queen smiled so big and so brightly
it made the king jump a little bit.
The queen handed the ruby to the king
and he stuffed it in his pocket.

The stories dictated by older preschool children often describe imaginary events.

put their hands together and use their optic beams to blink all the rest of the
teeth, twenty-five of them. Then they zoom out of the dinosaurs!

Benny, age 5

When offered the opportunity to dictate, children as old as eight or nine will
enthusiastically create complex stories. Many children enjoy dictating stories even
after they can read and write on their own. At this age, when their imaginations
often move more quickly than they can write, they may feel more comfortable
with the spoken than the written word. Unfortunately, most school-age children
rarely are offered the opportunity to dictate stories. In an ideal world, children
would continue to have the chance to dictate stories through third grade.

Common Themes

Although just about any subject, real or imaginary, can become the topic of a
child's story, common themes do emerge. For example, many children's stories
address emotional issues, such as conflict, or contain signs of their increasing
gender awareness. Children also may imitate stories they've heard, or tell the
same story over and over. Common themes often coincide with particular stages
of young children's cognitive development, and as that development progresses,
the themes become more complex and sophisticated.

Many dictated stories incorporate familiar language, characters, and images
from other sources, such as picture books, television, and songs. This is a natural
part of children's language acquisition.

I've been working on the railroad.

Lilly, age 3

Likewise, it's not unusual for children to retell familiar stories from books,
movies, or television. A child who retells a familiar story is trying out new vocabulary words and practicing how to put events in an ordered sequence. This is a
good way for children to learn the arc of a story: the characters are introduced, a
conflict or problem arises, and then the conflict or problem is resolved.

Alice falls into a deep hole. She falls and then she meets the rabbit. She
follows the rabbit. The rabbit was white. She goes through a lot of doors
that get smaller and smaller. She crawled through the last one. She couldn't
get through the door because she was too big. Then the dog said, "Try the

bottle on the table." It made her smaller and smaller and smaller until she
was the right size.

Linda, age 5

When a child tells the same story with the same characters over and over
again, it's usually because the story serves some function for him—for example,
he feels comforted by telling the same story over and over. You can nudge such
a child to expand his repertoire by introducing him to lots of different kinds of
stories and characters through storybooks, but it's also important to let him tell
different types of stories at his own pace.

Children's stories can contain lots of conflict. Sometimes the conflicts mirror
those the children face in their daily lives—sibling rivalry, for instance. Their stories also can be quite violent, describing shooting, bombs exploding, and death.
It's helpful to remember, if you're surprised by the violence in children's stories,
that their stories are not predictors of future behavior. (See chapter 11 for further
discussion of this topic.)

> Libby is always crazy. She hits May. She told her to stop it. And she told
> Mommy. Mommy said, "Please don't do that." Libby listened to Mommy.
> Libby kicked May. She poked her in the eye. May felt bad. Libby kicked
> and hit May again and May told Mommy again. Then May and Libby
> played together.
>
> *May, age 4*

You also may find a significant difference in content between the stories of girls
and those of boys. This difference is natural and expected. Children begin to show
gender awareness by the age of three, and they may try to explore expectations of
their gender roles through their play, including the stories they tell. Girls often
will tell stories about animals and fairytale characters, whereas boys are more likely
to tell stories about superheroes and monsters. (We discuss gender issues further
in chapter 12.)

One Child's Portfolio

Below we look at one child and how her stories developed from the time she
began dictating stories at age three until she entered kindergarten at age five.
Like those of many children, Keisha's first story was brief and focused on time
spent with her family.

> Mama and Papa and Keisha at the park. I slided down the slide and go up
> the ladder and slided down the slide.
>
> *Keisha, age 3*

As a four-year-old, Keisha created many stories related to her pretend play with her friends. We can see in these stories her growing cognitive abilities for abstraction. Keisha told the following story after she and her friend Rachel pretended they went camping together.

> Rachel and Keisha lived in a tent. They had a fire. They cooked their own
> food. They saw a bear but it was a nice bear. It gave them some honey.
>
> *Keisha, age 4*

As Keisha gained more experience dictating stories, her stories included more action, conflict, and poetic language.

> Once upon a time, a wind came blowing and blowing. Superbird came
> because there was danger and he saved me and Rachel. Then the sun came
> up and the curtains were blowing and blowing.
>
> *Keisha, age 4*

Keisha turned five the summer before she entered kindergarten. During that summer, Keisha frequently dictated stories and sometimes created elaborate drawings to accompany them. During this time, she also began incorporating dialogue into her stories. The following excerpt is from a longer story.

> Skink was a little bit naughty. He broke his mother's lamp down. It was a
> present from Skink's great-great-great-great aunt.
>   "My beautiful lamp! Why did you do that naughty thing, Skink?" said
> Skink's mom.
>   "I didn't do it! I don't know how it got broke!" said Skink.
>
> *Keisha, age 5*

Keisha's portfolio exemplifies the growth often exhibited by a child who enjoys dictating stories frequently. Keisha's early emphasis on her family and her later emphasis on imaginative stories and pretend play are representative of a pattern seen in many young children. Although not all children develop the ability to create stories with dialogue by the time they're five years old, it is generally true that the more experience of story dictation a child gains, the more sophisticated that child's stories become. Children's stories are shaped by their unique personality and interests, but the path for developing the skills of story dictation is generally the same for all children.

TEACHING TIPS

- Read to children a rich variety of storybooks, including folk tales, fairytales, and poetry. Expose children to imaginative ideas, language, and characters that challenge the predictable story lines they're likely to see on television.

- During story dictation, write down the children's words exactly as they say them. Do not be concerned about mistakes or things that are not logical. What a child decides is a story may look very different from the stories you're used to.

- Engage children in conversations about the stories they hear and the stories they tell. Help them discover the similarities and differences between stories. Children develop critical thinking skills when you encourage them to express personal opinions about what makes a good story.

- Be sure to save copies of children's dictated stories. You can then use them to document a child's growth and development over time.

PART 2

The Nuts and Bolts of Story Dictation

When I talk with early childhood teachers about story dictation, I'm frequently surprised by how many express feelings of doubt. Teachers wonder if they're doing story dictation "the right way." Or they wish they could do story dictation more often. Many teachers value and enjoy story dictation, but they sometimes struggle with making it a regular routine in their classrooms. Part II of this book is a practical guide for making story dictation happen regularly in any early childhood setting, from preschool classrooms to family child care homes.

In chapters 4 and 5, you'll find information on how to set up an area for story dictation, how to interact with children during story dictation, and how to include story dictation in your daily or weekly schedule. Chapter 6 describes how to use story dictation in an emergent curriculum and how to act out children's stories. In chapter 7, you'll find information on how to share stories with parents and families, and in chapter 8, you'll learn how to use story dictation to assess children's learning.

4

Story Dictation Basics

The care and education of young children is a very challenging responsibility. Early childhood providers must keep children safe, help them get along with each other, and prepare them to be successful in elementary school. Faced with divergent tasks ranging from helping children wash their hands to resolving disputes over toys to documenting the day's curriculum goals, providers don't have much time for squeezing in extra activities. The good news is that including story dictation in your program requires no squeezing. Rather, story dictation is an activity that will blend into your classroom and your daily routine, enriching and supporting what's already there. It may seem as if you are trying to add a new piece of furniture to an already crowded room, but the process is actually more like opening a window and letting in some fresh air.

This chapter explains the details of the story dictation process, such as where it takes place, who is involved, and how to include story dictation in your daily routines. You'll probably discover that you don't need additional equipment, time, or people to do it. To engage children in the story dictation process, you can use the resources you already have.

Setting the Stage for Story Dictation

Here's one scenario for incorporating story dictation in a typical preschool classroom.

It's time for free play, when children have their choice of a variety of table activities as well as playing in the block area or the dramatic play area. Several children sit together at a table with one teacher while they draw with crayons and markers. Some of these children are beginning to write the letters in their names or even those in their friends' names, while others simply draw shapes and lines. The children chat and laugh as they write and draw. A child who's sitting especially close to the teacher is speaking to the teacher while intensely watching the teacher's hand as she writes the child's words on the page. The teacher has positioned herself with her back to the wall so she's facing the room. Every few minutes, she looks around the room, taking stock of how the play is progressing and exchanging glances with her coteacher in the block area. After the first child finishes her story and leaves the table, another child moves his chair close to the teacher and begins his story.

Story dictation can be easily integrated into any classroom or child care environment. It requires few preparations, but before you get started, it's important that you set up a space for taking dictation, decide who will write down the children's stories, and develop some basic routines for classroom management.

Materials and Space

Although story dictation can occur just about anywhere, you may want to set up a table specifically for this activity. A preschool classroom typically has a writing or drawing table equipped with a tray of paper and a basket of crayons or markers. The difference here is that you want to create a space where the teacher can position herself at the table in order to listen to children's stories and write them down on paper.

Position the storytelling table so that the teacher sitting at it has a clear view of the room's other areas. A corner usually works best. The table should be placed away from heavy traffic and loud play, but it should be easily accessible to the children. Do not isolate the storytelling table in a nook or down a hall. If you do, children may forget it's there, making it less likely that they will spontaneously come over to tell a story. Stock the table with a stack of clean, unlined paper and some pencils. You may also want to include a basket of markers and crayons so children can illustrate their stories. These supplies will also help occupy the children who are waiting for a turn to dictate.

Keyboard or Pencil?

A writing table isn't the only place to do story dictation. I know some terrific teachers who use a computer keyboard. As a child tells her story, the teacher types the words directly into a computer file. That means she can save, format, and print stories as often as she pleases. Many teachers insist upon using a computer because they're afraid their handwriting isn't legible.

Although I believe that teachers should use whatever tools make the process work for them, I have to admit that I prefer pencil and paper. One reason is that I think the less equipment we use, the better the experience will be, because it minimizes distractions that might interrupt communication between me and the child. I find it much easier to convince a child that he has my full attention when I have only a slim piece of wood in my hand.

The other reason is less subtle. I think it's preferable that we use pencil and paper because one of the important functions of story dictation is to model writing behaviors. Many children learn new skills by watching others perform them. Most children will learn to write their first letters, words, and sentences not at a computer keyboard but by using a pencil. Children need to watch the tip of the pencil as it scrapes across the page and observe how the writer forms the curve of an *o* or the sharp angles of a *z*. Children need to smell the half-soapy, half-smoky aroma of an eraser rubbing against the paper. It's a sensory experience, and good early childhood environments provide a variety of sensory experiences to support learning.

Stories to Go

One necessity for writing down children's dictated stories is a hard surface on which to place the paper. That's the reason why story dictation usually occurs at a table. So maybe the person who invented the clipboard had early childhood providers in mind, because a clipboard allows story dictation to hit the road.

Armed with a clipboard, a teacher can take story dictation outdoors, on school buses, and into nap rooms and lunchrooms. Who knows where the muse will strike a child? The nature of these "stories to go" is much more spontaneous than that of stories written at a writing table. For example, during the bus ride home from a field trip to the zoo, you can pull out your clipboard and invite the children sitting near you to make up stories about the animals they've just seen.

> Once there was a lion. Its name was Flowers. He found lots of stores and
> then he buyed something.
> *Sheila, age 4*

Think about where your most interesting conversations with young children take place. At the snack table? in the bathroom while a child is sitting on the toilet? in the front hall at the end of the day, as you wait for the last parent to pick up her child? All these are wonderful settings for storytelling. Equipped with just a pencil, paper, and clipboard, teachers and child care providers can do story dictation just about anywhere a good conversation might take place.

The Scribe

In ancient Egypt, the scribe held a position of great honor. The same is true today in early childhood settings. Story dictation requires an attentive adult to sit quietly with a child and write down his stories. Ideally, the teacher who writes the story should be the child's primary caregiver, the one who has the strongest relationship with the child. As James Garbarino and Frances M. Stott note in their book *What Children Can Tell Us,* "when children are able to trust adults and feel protected by them, they're more willing to open up and express their innermost thoughts through play or storytelling" (1992, p. 165).

Since early childhood providers are very busy people who must constantly change directions throughout the day, sometimes the best way to make story dictation happen is to make use of assistants and volunteers. Appendix A of this book consists of a simple handout describing how to do story dictation. You are welcome to duplicate this handout and give it to volunteers who'll be writing down children's stories. One of the most important things volunteers or classroom assistants will need to know is that they should write down the child's words exactly as the child says them, without correcting the child's grammar or word choice.

Developing Routines for Classroom Management

As noted above, free play is usually an ideal time for offering story dictation as one of several interest areas. Story dictation works best when there is more than one teacher in the classroom, because listening to a child's story requires a teacher to give each storyteller one-on-one attention. So while one teacher floats about the room, making herself available where she is needed, another teacher stations herself at the writing table and takes dictation from the children.

This does not mean that the teacher who's taking dictation isn't also helping to supervise the classroom. The teacher taking dictation will need to pause occasionally to speak with other children and to communicate with the other teachers in the room. It may be helpful to think of writing down a child's story as similar to swimming underwater in a swimming pool: although you'll need to come up for air every minute or two, you'll still continue traveling, submerged, across the length of the pool.

Managing the classroom while one teacher is engaged with story dictation requires teamwork and good communication. Teachers must keep each other informed about what they're doing and what they need from each other. Suppose one teacher, Judy, is doing story dictation at a writing table, while the other teacher, Monique, is the floating teacher, moving to whatever area of the room needs the most attention. If a sudden demand, such as a child who has wet her pants, requires all of Monique's attention, Monique must let Judy know what's happening and ask for her help. "Judy," Monique might say, "Could you please watch the room while I help Denise?" Judy nods and says to the child who is dictating a story, "I need to stop for a minute, but I'll be right back. While you're waiting, maybe you could draw a picture of what's happening in your story." Judy stands and positions herself where she can better see the whole room. When Monique is ready to resume her position as the floater, Judy goes back to the writing table and finishes the child's story. Knowing that too many interruptions will stifle the flow of creative storytelling at the writing table, Monique and Judy work together to reduce the number of interruptions during story dictation by planning ahead for problems that might occur or by recruiting the assistance of other staff members or volunteers. Story dictation works best in a classroom with teachers like Judy and Monique, who value teamwork and are willing to support each other.

Introducing Story Dictation to the Children

Once you have prepared your classroom or child care environment for story dictation, you'll need to introduce this new activity to the children. The first time you offer individual story dictation, take a few minutes to introduce the idea to the children during a group meeting or at story time. You can tell them something like "Today you'll have a chance to try something new. You'll have a chance to tell a story, and I'll write down your story on a piece of paper so we can save it. You're welcome to come to the writing table today and have a turn to tell a story. Once your story is written down, we can read it again, anytime we like!"

Many children will already be familiar with the experience of having adults write down the words they say. Usually that experience takes place in a group. For example, during circle time, a teacher may post a large piece of paper on the wall and ask children to respond to questions, such as "What is your favorite food?" or "What do you like to do at the beach?" Each child has a turn, and the teacher writes the child's words where everyone can see. These kinds of group dictations can be done with children as young as two and are a wonderful introduction to the writing process. Teachers or child care providers may have written the children's words on holiday cards or on labels for their artwork. It's important that you help children understand that telling stories is different from writing a letter or answering questions. You may want to tell them that for this kind of story, they can use their imagination to say whatever they want to say. Explain to children that their stories can be about something pretend or something real. Make sure the children understand that they are in charge of what goes into their stories.

Although children will be excited about having the freedom to tell stories their own way, they may need a few ideas to help them get started. Invite children to tell stories about their families, their friends, or the things they like to do or play. You may also want to read aloud an example of a child's one-sentence story, such as

I like cake.

just to show them that a story can be very short.

The first day you offer story dictation, only a few children may be willing to try it. On the following day, take one or two of these first stories and read them aloud to the group, offering extravagant praise for the young pioneers who were brave enough to try something new. Gradually, over the course of many days or even weeks, more and more children will become excited about telling stories.

If there is a lull at the writing table during free play because children are involved in other interest areas, take a walk around the classroom and observe the children long enough to pinpoint what ideas and topics they're interested in that day. Then invite them to come to the writing table to talk about their interests and activities. For example, "When you're finished building that zoo out of blocks, maybe you'd like to tell a story about the animals." Or "When you're finished playing police station, maybe you'd like to tell a story about what happened to the robber." Invitations to tell stories that are based on children's pretend play will help to build a link between storytelling and the children's imaginations.

One of the most effective ways to motivate children to tell stories is to provide regular opportunities to act out, or dramatize, their stories. (We discuss this practice in more detail in chapter 6.) Children who've been reluctant to come to the writing table often become very enthusiastic about telling stories, once they understand that they and their friends can bring their story to life onstage. Another benefit to acting out stories is that children who are reluctant to tell their own stories can still participate in the process, as actors and audience members for other children's stories.

When story dictation is a choice, there will always be children who simply do not want to do it. That choice can be respected, but those children should still be regularly invited to participate. A sensitive teacher knows when to insist and when to honor a child's decision. In a quiet moment, you may ask the reluctant child, "How do you feel about telling stories? Is it something you might like to try?" Most likely the child will shrug and say, "I don't know." Offer some gentle suggestions. "Maybe you would enjoy telling a story if you had a friend to sit next to" or "Maybe you're not sure what to say." Perhaps the child needs an idea to get started: "Would you like to tell a story about a special time with your mommy?"

In classrooms where children are enthusiastic about dictating stories, an equitable system of taking turns can be implemented, such as keeping a list of children who want a turn. You may also want to post a sign-up sheet on which children can write their own names (with assistance, if needed) to indicate their interest in telling a story.

There will always be some children who dictate stories more frequently than others. Unless other children are missing out on their turns to tell stories, there is no reason to limit the number of stories a child can tell.

The Story Dictation Process

Once a child is seated at the table and ready, story dictation requires a "Yes?" look from you, the scribe, a look indicating that you are ready to listen and write. A "Yes?" look is an open and welcoming facial expression. You make eye contact, raise your eyebrows, and with your face give every indication that you are ready to offer the child your full attention.

Tell the child, "I'm ready to write down your story." Sometimes a child also needs to hear, "How does your story begin?" The child begins speaking, and you begin writing. Write down the child's words exactly as the child speaks them, adding punctuation as needed.

"I wonder" can be an enormously helpful phrase to use during interactions with children who are telling stories. Because a sentence that begins with this phrase is a statement rather than a question, the child is encouraged but not required to respond.

The following phrases may be useful at some point:

"I wonder how your story will begin."

"I wonder what will happen next in your story."

"I wonder what [name of a story character] is like."

"I wonder what else might happen in this story."

Embracing Mistakes

It is developmentally appropriate for young children, even those as old as five or six, to make frequent grammatical errors when they speak. For example, children often use incorrect forms of verbs. A child may say "goed" for "went" or "slided" for "slid" because he's learned that "-ed" at the end of a word indicates past tense. We can honor the logic behind these mistakes by allowing children to freely experiment with language without fear of correction.

Also, children often make mistakes in their use of pronouns, using "him" for "he" or even "he" for "she." Rather than correct a child, an action that might interrupt the flow of the child's ideas, look for opportunities to model the correct use of grammar. For example, if a child tells a story about a boy who "goed" to the park, you might remark, "I enjoyed hearing your story about the boy who went to the park." As children mature, they begin to notice the difference between the correct speech a teacher models and their own words.

During story dictation, the teacher or child care provider writes down the child's words exactly as the child says them.

> Rainbow bear got chased by a ghost. Her momma kill the ghost. Rainbow
> bear died. Her waked up. Her mommy feeled happy. Her big sister make
> her happy.
> *Sara, age 3*

When we compare a story a child dictated when she was three to one she dictated when she was five, we usually can see huge improvements in the child's grammar, as well as in vocabulary and sentence structure. When children have the opportunity to hear again the stories they told when they were younger, they're often amused by the grammatical mistakes they made and feel proud of the learning and progress they've made since that time.

Scaffolding Children's Learning

Children feel the most ownership and pride in their stories when adults refrain from directing them to tell stories a certain way. As teachers, our goal is to be as hands-off as possible during the dictation process. However, many children benefit from just enough support or scaffolding to provide the boost they need to progress as storytellers. Once children gain some experience in telling stories, a teacher's open-ended questions, used sparingly, can help guide children in learning to become better storytellers.

For example, although young children usually do a very good job of creating or choosing characters for their stories, they're often not very good at adding actions or plot. Children may need a little prompting to make something happen in their stories. Perhaps a child begins a story by saying "There was a princess and a puppy" and then seems unsure about how to proceed. The teacher can then ask an open-ended question, such as, "What happens to the princess and the puppy?" or "What do the princess and the puppy do?" The same strategy can be used when a child tells a true story about real people. A child begins a story by saying, "My daddy took me to the park." The teacher can ask, "What happened at the park?"

In some ways, the teacher's task during story dictation is to clear a path between the child and the paper. Teachers who are successful at developing creative storytelling in their classrooms know how to disappear. They know there should be as few intrusions as possible between the child and the paper so that the child's language, emotions, and thinking can authentically appear on the page. The story then emerges like a photographic image that develops before your eyes.

Ending a Story

When a child is finished telling a story, she might say, "That's it" or "The end." But it's often difficult to know whether the child has completed her story or has stopped for some other reason. Perhaps she isn't sure what happens next, or she's been distracted by something else going on in the room. At this point, it may be helpful to read back to the child the words that you've written down. Then pause and give the child your best "Yes?" look.

Or, when a child doesn't continue with his story, ask, "Is there anything else you'd like to add?" If his answer is no, the story is finished. Sometimes children, especially those with a great deal of storytelling experience, are reluctant to end their stories. They could continue for pages and pages. For this reason, it's a good idea to limit stories to one page each. During dictation, if your writing has just about filled the page, say to the child, "Look, there's only a little bit of room left on the paper. Can you think of a way to end your story?"

Illustrations

Sometimes a story begins as a picture a child has drawn, although the child may not have had a story in mind when she began the drawing. For young children, drawing is a process, a sensory experience. This is especially true of very young children, two or three years old, when they're first learning to draw. If you ask the child, "What did you make?" he may not be able to answer you. But if you say, "Tell me about your picture," he may be able to describe the shapes and colors he sees. These dictated words can be written on the same page as the drawing or on a separate piece of paper. The child's description of his drawing becomes his story.

Some children talk while they're drawing, telling a story to themselves as they add layer upon layer of color and lines to the page. A teacher sitting next to such a child can write down these words on a separate piece of paper, capturing the excitement of the story in the drawing as it unfolds.

Older preschool children, such as four- and five-year-olds, may be able to plan their drawings ahead of time. Children at this age, who are just beginning to develop the ability to create recognizable figures, such as people with heads, features, arms, and legs, may be quite eager to tell stories about what they've drawn.

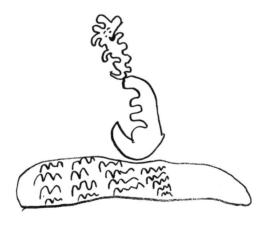

This is water. A boat in the water. In the top is a cat.

The dictated words can be written onto the same page as the child's drawing, or the child may want to do his own writing.

Some children are interested in adding illustrations after a story has been written, to make their story look more like the picture books they're accustomed to seeing in the classroom, at the library, and at home. Teachers can facilitate the illustration process by typing the words of the child's story into a word processing file and printing out pages with just a sentence or two of text at the bottom of each page. The child can then add illustrations. Usually only older preschoolers have the attention span and patience to complete more than two or three illustrations for a single story. Because there's a broad range of interest and ability among preschool children when it comes to illustrating stories, this works best as an option for individual children who have a special passion for the task.

Children intuitively understand that there is a meaningful, almost magical connection between words and pictures. Sometimes a story inspires a drawing. Sometimes a drawing inspires a story. Like the chicken and the egg, it may be impossible to determine which comes first. Although professional authors and illustrators will agree that sometimes the images come first, and sometimes the words do, they'll also tell you that sometimes they're so closely connected it feels as if they were created simultaneously. Creating their own stories allows children the opportunity to express and explore their passions, imaginations, and creativity.

Illustrating stories does help children make connections between images and text, but illustrations aren't always necessary. In fact, it's important that children also have occasional experiences with print without illustrations so they can learn that print alone carries meaning.

Story Dictation in Family Child Care and Homeschooling

Story dictation can be practiced in a family child care environment in much the same way it is practiced in a classroom. A caregiver sits at a table or on the floor with a clipboard and asks the child, "How does your story begin?" Since children in family child care are often cared for in mixed-age groups, story dictation is a good way to challenge and engage an older child, such as a preschooler who's in a group with toddlers or infants. As the older child dictates stories to a caregiver, she becomes a role model for the younger children, who will soon want to dictate stories of their own. However, as described earlier, story dictation requires giving full attention to one child, which can be very difficult to do in a family child care setting, where one caregiver often works in isolation. Although creating time in the daily schedule for story dictation may take some careful planning, it is well worth the effort. Fortunately, story dictation is a quiet activity that requires very little preparation, so it can be done while younger children are napping or engaging in play.

Dictation is a familiar practice among homeschooling families, who often use it to teach children literacy skills up to a third- or fourth-grade level. One reason is that many homeschool curriculum materials are inspired by Charlotte Mason, a teacher who lived in England from 1842 to 1923. Mason promoted the dictation of narratives as the optimal way to teach reading and writing. In addition to taking dictation from children, Mason also saw value in children taking dictation from adults as a means of practicing spelling and punctuation (Krueger).

The story dictation processes described in homeschooling curriculum materials are usually much more structured and adult-directed than the methods described in this book. For example, one popular curriculum advises that children create each element of a story—such as the setting, the problem, and the conclusion—separately (Joel and Simonson 1996). This may be because these practices are often used with school-age children who are ready to formally study the conventions of storytelling. Regardless of what methods a homeschooling parent chooses to use for teaching reading and writing, the open-ended story dictation practices described in this book can be used among preschool-age children as an introduction to the more formal writing practices they will learn later.

TEACHING TIPS

● Make time in your routine for regular story dictation. Offering story dictation as a choice during free play usually works best.

● While one teacher is engaged in story dictation, the teachers must work together as a team to ensure that the classroom is well supervised. The teacher taking dictation should pause between stories to check in with the other teachers and monitor what's going on in the room.

● Write down the child's words exactly as the child speaks them. Do not make any changes in the child's grammar or word choice.

● Resist the temptation to edit or censor stories that contain strong language or violent images. (We discuss this issue at length in chapter 13.)

5

Story Dictation in Groups

Working with a group of young children is a little like trying to pat your head and rub your belly at the same time. You have to constantly balance the individual needs of the children with the demands of group management. This chapter describes how story dictation, which requires short spells of individual attention, fits into either small-group or large-group activities. With a little planning and organization, you'll find that you can manage a group of children and still provide the individual attention that is necessary for story dictation.

Working with Small Groups of Children

As described in the previous chapter, story dictation usually works well as a choice during free play. With this structure, a small group, perhaps three to six children, gathers at a writing or art table to draw, write, and take turns dictating stories. Participation in the small group can be voluntary, with children coming and going as they please, or teachers can assign children to a specific small group and then call each group, one at a time, to the table on a rotating basis.

When children gather in small groups for story dictation, their interactions create wonderful opportunities for developing friendships, building language skills, practicing conflict resolution, and sharing ideas and information. Let's look closely at one typical scene at a writing table in a preschool classroom.

Maya, age four, is dictating a story to the teacher, Ms. Abby. Two other four-year-olds, Antoine and Jasmine, are coloring at the table.

"How does your story begin, Maya?" Ms. Abby asks.

"Once there was a witch," Maya begins. "She had an ugly dog."

Antoine and Jasmine laugh at Maya's word choice. Maya smiles, pleased that her friends have noticed the humor in her words.

"It was the ugliest dog in the whole world!" Maya exclaims. Ms. Abby continues to write Maya's words.

"Look, Jasmine," says Antoine, pointing at his picture. "I'm drawing an ugly dog."

A younger child, three-year-old Devin, wanders over to the table. He stands a few feet away, watching and listening.

Maya peeks over at Antoine's drawing. "That dog isn't ugly, Antoine. My dog is much uglier than that." The children laugh.

Antoine says, "Put that in your story, Maya. Say that your dog is uglier than mine."

Ms. Abby asks Maya, "What do you think, Maya? Do you want me to write that in your story? That your dog was much uglier than Antoine's?"

Maya nods. "But it isn't my dog, it's the witch's dog. In the story."

Ms. Abby asks, "So should I write, 'The witch's dog was much uglier than Antoine's dog'?"

Maya nods. "The dog was so ugly"—Maya glances at her friends and smiles—"and stinky"—on cue, Antoine and Jasmine laugh—"that everybody was screaming. Everybody was holding their noses. Everybody covered their eyes and said, 'Yuck! That dog is disgusting!'" Antoine and Jasmine continue to laugh at Maya's words, and Maya smiles broadly as she watches their response.

Devin continues to watch from a few feet away. He doesn't smile or laugh, but his full attention is focused on the children at the story table. Maya finishes her story. As Ms. Abby reads it back, the three children laugh again. When Maya is finished, she and Antoine and Jasmine leave the table and begin playing in the block area. Ms. Abby turns to Devin, who's still standing in the same place.

"Would you like to tell a story, Devin?" Ms. Abby asks.

Devin nods shyly. He sits down next to the teacher. This is Devin's first time telling a story.

"How does your story begin, Devin?" Ms. Abby asks.

"Stinky dog! Ugly dog!" Devin exclaims, grinning. Ms. Abby writes down Devin's words. She looks at Devin and waits. Devin just smiles with satisfaction.

"Is there anything else you want to add to your story, Devin?" Devin shakes his head. "This sounds like a story that Maya and Antoine and Jasmine might like, doesn't it?" Devin nods enthusiastically.

Stories and Social Interaction

In this example, a number of social exchanges—all inspired by the storytelling process—are going on. Maya is clearly creating a story that she thinks her friends at the table will enjoy and appreciate. She is gratified by their response, and their laughter inspires her to further develop the humor in her story. In turn, Maya's story inspires Antoine to draw a picture of an ugly dog. Perhaps later he'll tell his own story about an ugly dog. Although Maya doesn't think the dog Antoine drew was uglier than the one in her story, she nevertheless incorporates his picture into her story by saying that the dog in her story is "much uglier" than the dog that Antoine drew.

Another important social interaction illustrated here is that the older children have served as role models for Devin, the younger child who watches the exchange. Some teachers (and parents) might think that a silly discussion about a dog that makes use of negative terms like ugly or stinky is an inappropriate model for a younger child. Perhaps it's not ideal, but look at the result. From watching the interactions around Maya's ugly dog story, Devin finds the courage and inspiration to come to the story table for the first time. He obviously enjoyed the silly humor of Maya's story and saw the power the story had to capture the attention of the other children. The storytelling process has inspired these children to pay attention to each other, collaborate, cooperate, communicate, form or deepen friendships, and make emotional connections.

Conversations and interactions at the story table are wonderful things, but when the conversations get lively, the teacher must ensure that the author of the story retains the authority to determine its course. Other children can make suggestions and offer ideas, but when a child is dictating, she should be the sole author. The teacher, or scribe, should check in with the author after each suggestion by asking, "Do you like that idea? Do you want those words added to your story?" or "Is that something you want in your story, or should he save that idea for his own story?"

Collaboration and social interaction at the story table provide a unique opportunity for quiet or timid children to offer and receive ideas. In other settings, such as on the playground, the bigger, louder, and stronger children often dominate. But at the story table, all have the chance to participate.

Children usually offer ideas and suggestions spontaneously, but a teacher may also invite specific input. If, for example, a child is having trouble thinking of an ending for her story, the teacher may facilitate the offering of suggestions—while also encouraging the building of partnerships and collaboration—by saying, "Lori isn't sure how to end her story. Does anyone have an idea?" Or when a child comes to the story table with a strong desire to tell a story but doesn't seem to know how to begin, the teacher may say to other children nearby, "You all know Bryan pretty well. What does Bryan like to play? What does he like to pretend about?" Children who have experience engaging in pretend play with the child (Bryan, in this case) become an important resource and usually can offer good suggestions.

Other Ways to Do Story Dictation in Small Groups

Rather than offering story dictation during free choice, you can offer it during small-group activity time, when the whole class is divided into several smaller groups that are each in a different area of the room. This option works well when there are enough teachers or volunteers to provide an adult for every four or five children. In these small groups, children can take turns telling individual stories. As described earlier, you can invite children to draw a picture while they wait for a turn to dictate a story. Or the children can dictate a story together, with each child having a turn to add a phrase or sentence. Sometimes teachers structure these small-group writing activities by asking children to retell a story they've recently heard read aloud, perhaps a familiar story or fairytale like *The Three Little Pigs* or *The Gingerbread Man*. Some children enjoy this structure, while others prefer the freedom to make their own choices about such things.

> The lady and the cow and the man were chasing the gingerbread man.
> Then the fox came. He said, "Can I take you for a ride on the water?" Then
> all the people couldn't chase him now.
> *Randi, age 4*

Small groups, whether formed spontaneously during play or organized by a teacher, are ideal for story dictation. Gathering children in small groups encourages conversation and collaboration. I've found that when children gather in mixed-age small groups, including children as young as three and as old as five, the opportunities for learning are especially rich. The younger children learn from the older children and the older children gain confidence because they enjoy serving as role models.

Using Journals with Large Groups of Children

Sustaining the attention of a large group of preschoolers, such as a typical class of eighteen to twenty children, is very difficult. In early childhood classrooms, large-group activities usually require children to sit still, wait, and listen—things that most three- to five-year-olds just cannot do for any length of time. With the right planning and organization, however, story dictation can indeed work as a large-group activity. One way to manage the activity is to seat children at tables and make story dictation part of a classroom journaling time.

Assign each child in the class a spiral notebook to be used as a journal. During a special time each day, such as the time between free play and outdoor play, the children sit at tables with a basket of markers or crayons at the center of each table. The teachers pass out the journals, which are labeled with each child's name. The children are then invited to draw or "write" whatever they choose on the pages of their journals.

Working in individual journals is an excellent way for children to practice their developing writing skills. Young children learn to write by developing the dexterity to form small lines and curves and acquiring an understanding of letters, words, and text. They develop writing skills through practice, such as drawing and writing in their journals, and through experiences with the printed word.

When children as young as two or three are invited to "write," they usually scribble in a controlled pattern that may include small circles or wavy lines. Although they don't yet know how to write letters and words, these scribbles are distinctly different from the broad lines and large shapes they create when they're invited to draw a picture. The controlled scribbles of these two- and three-year-olds are their first attempts to imitate print. As they get older and gain more practice, they'll develop the ability to copy a specific letter, such as the first letter in their own names. Eventually, around the time they turn five, they'll develop the ability to write all the letters in their first name (Baghban 2007).

Children may simply use their journals to practice "writing," but sometimes they may need a prompt or a question to help them think of something to draw or write. You can suggest to a child that she draw or write about someone she loves or about her favorite thing to do at the park.

As the children draw, write, or scribble in their notebooks, teachers can circulate among the group, taking dictation from one child at a time. This works best when you can have a teacher at each table. The teacher sits in a low chair next to the child and writes the child's words directly onto the journal page. Some children will have a preference about where in their journal the teacher should write. For example, a child who's worked hard on a drawing may not want the teacher to write words in the middle of it. Ask the child, "May I write your words here?" and point to the space where you plan to write.

Before the children's first session with their journals, you may want to think carefully about how formal and structured you'd like this activity to be. Some teachers of older preschoolers (such as four- and five-year-olds) ask the children to write their names, as best they can, at the beginning of each new journaling session. Also decide whether it's important to you that children use the pages in order, from front to back. If it is, you'll have to teach the children to do this, because most young children select pages at random. They must be shown how to find the front cover, open it, and turn the pages one by one until they find the next blank page. Five-year-olds and some older four-year-olds will be able to learn this, but three-year-olds and young four-year-olds may have a difficult time and probably should be allowed to use pages at random.

Keep in mind that there will naturally be a wide variety in the children's attention spans. Some could journal all day. For others, a few minutes will be enough. It's best to keep the activity short, ten minutes or less, and then make sure the journals are available at other times of the day so that children with more interest can continue their journaling later.

> The dinosaurs went to the sun. The sun gave the dinosaurs five things to
> wish. The dinosaurs went away. They said, "Thank you." They saw the guy
> in the whirlpool. The guy said, "Stop the whirlpool." The whirlpool flushed

him down. The guy came back. He said, "I like to be down there!" But then
he decided to come back anyway.

Jill, age 4

Journal entry

Whether the groups are large or small, children benefit from the opportunity
to listen to and respond to each other's stories. Children's stories are frequently
inspired by conversations with their friends and classmates. The desire to engage
and entertain other children helps motivate storytellers. Having children practice
story dictation in groups is both a necessity for classroom management and an
opportunity for learning and social interaction.

TEACHING TIPS

- Allow children to engage in spontaneous conversations during
  the story dictation process. Talking with other children can be
  a source of inspiration for the storyteller and can lead to collaboration.

- Remember that your role as teacher during these conversations is to gently guide the conversation so that the child
  who is dictating maintains control over the story. Turn to the
  storyteller frequently and say, "Do you like that idea?" or "Is
  that the way you want your story to go?"

- Inexpensive spiral notebooks make great journals that children
  can use for drawing, scribbling, dictating stories, and attempt-
  ing to write actual letters. Keep these journals on a low shelf
  so children can use them at any time.

6

Building on Children's Stories

Learning, of course, doesn't stop with capturing a child's story on paper. Early childhood providers can use dictated stories to enrich their curriculum, build a positive classroom environment, and support the development of critical thinking skills among the children in their care. This chapter begins with a guide to using dictated stories to inspire, shape, and enrich early childhood curricula, especially "emergent" curriculum models that are based on children's interests. Next, we take a close look at dramatizing children's stories, an activity that makes children's words come alive, encourages positive social interactions, and is surprisingly simple to do. Finally, this chapter presents ideas for using children's dictated stories to promote problem solving and critical thinking skills.

The Role of Children's Dictated Stories in Curriculum Development

Dictated stories can play an important role in curriculum models that are built around investigating a specific topic and that emphasize ongoing documentation of children's learning. These models, many of which are inspired by the Reggio Emilia schools in Italy, are usually described as having a project approach. The topic is often "emergent," meaning the idea for it has been selected by the teachers because they've gathered evidence, usually by observing children's play, that the children are interested in the topic and will find it meaningful and engaging. Based on what the children are most curious about, the teachers help the children develop their own questions to investigate. Many early childhood educators enjoy using the project approach because it is based on current research about how children learn, it is developmentally appropriate, and it allows opportunities for creativity.

One of the best ways to use dictated stories as part of an emergent curriculum is to use the content and topics of the stories to help identify children's interests. A teacher might, for example, notice that many children in the class are telling stories about dinosaurs.

> Dinosaurs were alive a long time ago. They were all over the place. They
> left their bones for us.
> *Scott, age 5*
>
> Two dinosaurs were fighting. The one had teeth that were the biggest teeth.
> It ate the other dinosaur.
> *Brian, age 4*

Once teachers notice a trend in story topics, the next step is to initiate conversations with the children about their stories and to learn what it is about the topic that has captured their interest. Such conversations can be formal and structured, or informal and loose, or a combination of both. During group time, teachers can gather information formally by asking the children what they know about dinosaurs and documenting their responses on large sheets of paper.

As mentioned in chapter 4, it's important to help children distinguish between telling a creative story and answering a specific question. You can make this distinction by explaining that stories come from their imagination, whereas talking about a specific topic is simply writing down answers to questions you ask them. To further distinguish these two kinds of dictation, you may find it helpful to do story dictation in one place, such as the writing table, and do writing down answers in another place, such as the rug, where you write the words on large sheets of paper.

In the case of the dinosaur stories, the teacher, Ms. Deana, began gathering information during an informal conversation at the lunch table.

Teachers can document what children know about a topic by writing down their answers to questions.

Ms. Deana: *"I've noticed that many of you have been telling stories about dinosaurs lately. I wonder why so many children like to think about dinosaurs."*

Scott: *"I like dinosaurs."*

Anna: *"I like dinosaurs too."*

Ms. Deana: *"What do you like about dinosaurs?"*

Brian: "They're big! Rrraar!"
Anna: "I like all their bones."
Ms. Deana: "Their bones?"
Scott: "I saw dinosaur bones at the museum. My daddy took me."
Brian: "Me too! I saw dinosaur bones!"
Anna: "Me too! The bones are really old. Older than me."
Scott: "Older than anybody."
Brian: "Yeah. And their teeth are old too."

Through conversations like this, Ms. Deana learned that what interested the children most were the bones and teeth of dinosaurs. During a planning meeting with her teaching team, Ms. Deana suggested they begin a unit on dinosaurs, with a focus on fossils and dinosaur bones. The other teachers agreed, and the team planned curriculum activities for the following week that were related to dinosaurs and their bones. For example, they began the week by reading aloud from the book *Digging Up Dinosaurs* by Aliki and by hiding plastic dinosaur bones in the sandbox that children could dig up during outdoor play.

Once a topic for investigation has been chosen, you also can use dictated stories and narratives to document children's ongoing learning and interests during the course of the project. You may be tempted to direct the children to dictate stories that are related to the project, but do not restrict their choices. Continue to allow children to tell stories any way they please. If a project has really captured the interest and imagination of the children, there will be a natural increase in dictated stories related to the project topic.

The curriculum activities in Ms. Deana's dinosaur unit did indeed add to the children's knowledge about dinosaurs and their bones. Ms. Deana could see the evidence in the children's dictated stories. For example, some of the children began using the names of specific dinosaurs.

The brachiosaurus was playing. Then the triceratops. They said, "Let's play together!"
Brooke, age 4

Ms. Deana and her teaching team used the new stories to plan and shape the rest of the dinosaur unit. They decided to build on the children's new knowledge of dinosaur names by helping the children explore the differences between the skeletons of dinosaurs from different genera. Ms. Deana found books with large pictures of the skeletons of dinosaurs at the library. The teachers displayed these pictures at the art table and invited the children to create their own dinosaur skeletons, using pipe cleaners, wire, and clay. The teachers also read aloud Jan Wahl's book *The Field Mouse and the Dinosaur Named Sue*. As a result of activities like these, the children began to recognize characteristics of different dinosaurs. Their new learning was soon reflected in many of their dictated stories.

> Once there were some dinosaurs. The tyrannosaurus was the meanest. His name was Rex. There was a triceratops too. His name was Tops. But Tops wasn't afraid of Rex. "My three horns are bigger than your teeth. I'm going to scare you away." And he did.
>
> *Logan, age 5*

> The scientists were digging and digging. They got hot and dirty. Then one of the scientists said, "Eureka!" They found a brontosaurus bone. Everybody cheered. They brought the bone back to the museum.
>
> *Sofia, age 5*

Documenting Children's Learning

Sharing children's dictated stories with the class helps them reflect on their learning. You may read children's stories aloud during group time to discuss a particular topic or idea. Children can be influenced or inspired by the thinking of others when they hear what other children have said. The stories (as well as the narratives children dictate together during group time) can also be used to compare old ideas to new ones. Ms. Deana was able to ask one of her students, "Remember when you said that some dinosaurs are still alive? Do you still think that, or do you think something else now?"

Dictated stories also play an important role in assessing children's learning at the end of a project. When Ms. Deana wrote her assessment at the conclusion of the dinosaur unit, she compared the children's early stories about dinosaurs to their more recent ones. She was able to use the stories as evidence of the children's progress, such as the increase in their vocabulary and their new understanding of the role of a scientist. To assess the learning of children who didn't make up their own dinosaur stories, Ms. Deana used sources, such as dictated narratives, that answered direct question like "What do you know about dinosaurs?" as well as her observations of the children's play.

Ms. Deana's dinosaur unit illustrates how dictated stories and narratives can play a role at every stage in the development of an emergent curriculum. Although there are many ways to identify and develop engaging curriculum topics (recording observations of children's pretend play is one), story dictation is an especially fruitful practice because it generates pieces of documentation that can be used to assess and reflect upon children's learning.

Acting Out Stories

One of the best ways to build on and share stories while developing a strong sense of community in your classroom is to act them out or dramatize them. Dramatization usually occurs during large-group or circle time. The teacher gathers the children together, the roles in the story are assigned to individual children, and the young author of the story stands in front of the group. The teacher reads the story aloud, pausing after each sentence or action to allow the children to act out the events or actions in the story.

In this section, as we guide you through the basics of dramatization, we will explore in some depth the benefits of acting out children's stories.

The actors listen carefully as the teacher reads the story.

Benefits of Acting Out the Stories

Many teachers who practice story dictation in their own classrooms insist that acting out the stories is an essential part of the story dictation process. They've learned that acting out the stories is consistent with a core principle of developmentally appropriate practice: children learn best from hands-on experiences. When children act out stories, they see, hear, touch, move, and speak, making the story a concrete, physical experience.

Another benefit is that once they have experience in acting out stories, children become better storytellers. They begin to understand how to use words to create action and to complete an idea. They can imagine as they're telling their story how it will look acted out. My experience has been that children are more likely to use action words and to include dialogue when they know their stories will later be acted out.

The process of acting out a story is an opportunity for collaboration. For example, as they're acting out the story, children may discover ambiguities or problems that need to be solved. Exactly how many monsters are in that closet? Where does the bird fly to? The teacher can ask the author open-ended questions, and the rest of the class may offer ideas and input. The story develops and changes as a result of being acted out.

Acting out stories also is likely to inspire children who've been reluctant to create stories in the past. Because acting out stories makes abstract ideas more accessible, it is particularly recommended for young children who are English-language learners or children who, for whatever reason, have difficulty communicating through words. Imagine, for example, explaining to a child who doesn't speak English that her friend has been away on vacation. You might say, "Kaylee went on a trip. She was visiting her relatives in California." Now imagine that same child sitting in the audience as this simple story is briefly dramatized:

> One time I went on American Airlines. I went to California. I played with
> my cousin. We played trains.
> *Kaylee, age 3*

The child hears the teacher read the story as the narrator, Kaylee, stands before the group and spreads out her arms like an airplane and runs around the rug. Then a child who's been assigned the role of the cousin steps forward, and she and Kaylee kneel on the floor and pretend to roll a train back and forth. A child needn't be the author of a story to benefit from seeing it acted out. Children who are actors in a story or are part of the audience also benefit from seeing words on a page come to life.

When stories are acted out, they begin to have more meaning and emotional power for the children. Gillian Dowley McNamee of the Erikson Institute, who coauthored *Early Literacy,* has said, "From the child's perspective, there is simply no point in telling a story unless it is to be acted out" (G. McNamee, pers. comm.).

Classroom Management and Acting Stories Out

Teachers may be reluctant to let children act out stories because they're afraid doing so will take up too much time. The truth is that acting out a child's story takes only about ninety seconds. Another reason teachers are reluctant to act out stories is because they're afraid of losing control of the children. I know this is possible, because it happened to me.

My first teaching job was as an assistant kindergarten teacher in a small private school. One fall day, early in the school year, the head teacher was absent due to illness. Even though I had very little training and experience and no time to prepare, I was put in charge of the class. And the aide called in from the office to assist me had even less classroom experience than I did. Hoping to engage the children in a really fun activity, I decided the class would act out one of their favorite picture books, Maurice Sendak's *Where the Wild Things Are.* I let all twenty-two children decide whether they wanted to be Max or a Wild Thing, and, as I read the story aloud, I encouraged everyone to stand up and act out what was happening on the page. I cringe now as I remember how the situation quickly got out of hand, especially as the Wild Things began to "roar their terrible roars." Soon half the class was running around the room and the other half was in tears. I had to abruptly end the activity and order everyone back to the safety of their own seats.

One of the several important lessons I learned that day was that acting out stories can be an emotionally intense experience. Stories can be frightening to children, and books like *Where the Wild Things Are* inspire strong emotions. That's why it's a good idea to practice acting out stories from familiar, comforting picture books and fairytales like Ruth Krauss's *The Carrot Seed,* Esphyr Solbedkina's *Caps for Sale,* John Burningham's *Mr. Gumpy's Outing,* and David Shannon's *Duck on a Bike.* (See Appendix C for additional titles). Once the children have had some successful experiences acting out simple picture books, they'll be ready to act out their own stories.

The Teacher's Role as Stage Manager

My embarrassing fiasco with *Where the Wild Things Are* also taught me that the teacher has to take an active role in directing and managing the dramatization of stories. Acting out stories cannot be a free-for-all. When adult actors perform, they need a stage manager to keep things running smoothly. The same is true for young children. The teacher takes on the role of stage manager, providing the direction and structure that will keep the group safe and orderly. When done well, acting out a story is a carefully orchestrated performance.

Begin by clearly defining the space for the stage, which needn't be larger than five feet by eight feet. What you must have is clear boundaries around the edges that children can see. A rectangular rug works well, or you can use masking tape to mark off the stage and the areas where children can sit. There's no need to worry about a front or back to this performance space; children in the audience can sit along all sides of the performance area.

Limiting the size of the stage is one way that you, as stage manager, create structure and control. With a small, clearly defined performance space, only a small number of actors can perform at one time. Luckily, most children's stories have only a handful of characters anyway. Should a child write a story about, for example, twelve dancing bunnies, you would help the young author adapt her story for the stage by reducing the number of dancing bunnies to three.

Begin the acting-out session by inviting the author to stand next to you. Read the story aloud once and then announce which characters are needed. In some cases, you and the author will already have discussed this at the story table, after the story was dictated.

Suppose the story to be acted out was this one:

> Once there was a witch. She was cooking her stew. Then she heard a knock at the door. It was her friend Emily with her baby, Lily. Emily took off Lily's diaper to change it. Then she put her clothes back on her. The stew was done. They ate some of it. It was yummy. Lily cried because she was tired.
> Jordan, age 4

You would first announce that the characters in the story are a witch, Emily, and baby Lily. The author always gets first choice of which role to play. If the author doesn't wish to play a role, that's also fine. Let's say that the author of this story, Corinne, decides to be the witch. You then assign roles in the order the children are seated. You offer the first child the role of Emily, which she gladly takes. You offer the next child the role of baby Lily. Each child has the option of refusing the role and passing it to the next child. No one is forced to play a role. At the same time, roles are offered in a systematic fashion, without playing favorites, so everyone has the opportunity to participate.

As teacher, you may also suggest that an actor play an inanimate object in the story. For this story, you might ask author Corinne if she'd like someone to be the stew. Since no real props or scenery are used, this is a fun way to make a story a bit more interesting. It also challenges the children to use their imaginations. How does one pretend to be a stew?

With the roles of all the characters assigned, the acting out of the story can begin. You read the first line of the story and pause, allowing time for the action. If needed, you give stage directions.

Once there was a witch.

Corinne steps forward. At this point, if the children have already had some experience with acting out stories, you might challenge Corinne, as author and actor, to think about the character of the witch. Perhaps you'd ask, "What kind of witch are you? Are you a young witch or an old witch? Can you show us with your face and your body what kind of witch you are?"

You continue reading, pausing after each line or couple of lines, to allow the actors to show the words of the story.

She was cooking her stew.

(The child who plays the stew crouches down on the floor. The witch moves her hand above the child, pretending to stir.)

Then she heard a knock on the door. It was her friend Emily with her baby, Lily.

(The children playing Emily and Lily step forward.)

Emily took off Lily's diaper to change it. Then she put her clothes back on her.

Any mention of a diaper in a child's story is probably going to cause giggling and silliness. This is fine. It means the children are paying attention and are engaged in the story. As stage manager, you must keep the momentum of the story moving forward. It's usually best just to keep going and let the story play out, rather than try to stop and calm the children down. As another part of being stage manager, you have to maintain a matter-of-fact attitude about the events in a story.

The stew was done. They ate some of it. It was yummy.

(You might need to direct the witch to serve the soup to her guests before they can eat it.)

Lily cried because she was tired.

(The child playing Lily says, "Wah!" and wipes her eyes.)

You bring the story to a close by saying "The end." Some teachers may choose to invite the actors to take a bow while the audience applauds, but this is not necessary. In the interest of saving time for more stories, you may want to keep bowing and applauding to a minimum.

Many children feel a little shy when performing in a story, and their actions and movements may be quite small. For example, a child may represent eating stew simply by moving his hand toward his mouth. This is fine. After all, the purpose of acting out stories is not to train children to become thespians.

Managing Violent and Scary Scenes

Some children's stories contain a great deal of fighting and other violence, enough so that children may be tempted to actually kick or hit each other. Are we to allow children to pretend to fight? In some cases, the answer is yes, but only with very specific controls.

If a story contains fighting and the child wants the story acted out, you, as the teacher, are justified in taking steps to direct the action to ensure everyone's safety. This may even include making changes to the story. Your role in the acting out of a story is significantly different from your role as scribe during the initial dictation. Children should be allowed a great deal of freedom to express their ideas when they're dictating their stories, but the same isn't necessarily true for the acting out of stories. You, not the child, must direct story dramatization.

Sometimes you will need to help a child edit a story to make it suitable for its audience, perhaps by changing the ending of a violent story to something more peaceful. When this is necessary, you should explain to the young author what changes have to be made and why. Such a conversation can take place in advance, at the writing table, after the story has been written and before it is acted out. You might say, "This story is really important. I'm glad you told it. But your story may scare some of the children, so if we're going to act it out with the rest of the class, we'll have to make some changes." Communicate to the child that not acting out a story is also an acceptable choice. Some stories are not meant to be shared with the whole group, and we can respect a child's choice in the matter.

If the violence in a story is mild and you don't think children in the audience will be frightened or harmed by seeing it, you can have the children act it out using pretend fighting, in which physical contact is not made. After one quick lesson and a demonstration of pretend fighting, most children easily understand how to perform it safely. In fact, children are usually able to understand very quickly that the stage for acting out stories is a special place with special rules. From the child's point of view, there is much to be gained from following the rules and performing stories safely. They are personally invested in their own stories and the stories of their friends. They want to see them performed and are motivated to do what is required to make that happen.

Here's an example of a story that contains a lot of fighting.

> First there were two bad guys. And then they could change invisible. Then there were knight children. They could fight. They had guns and swords to fight the bad guys.
> *Daniel, age 4*

After the roles of bad guys and knight children have been assigned, you might say to the children, "Do you know how to pretend to fight with guns and swords? You have to do it without touching each other. Can you do that?" You might ask one child to demonstrate.

Teachers who regularly act out children's stories will tell you that dramatizing stories is very satisfying to children. In fact, acting out stories gives children so much pleasure that they become motivated to follow directions and stay within a teacher's guidelines. Teachers frequently comment that children who often become restless and disruptive during traditional story time behave appropriately and become very engaged when the class acts out stories written by the children

Andrew's Story

This is a story about an eating plane. He eats a lightning bolt. Then he eats another and another and another one. He explodes.

The End.

Plane — Matthew
Lightning Bolt - Andrew
Lightning Bolt - Lauren
Lightning Bolt - Max

To save time, some teachers write a list of the roles in a story right on the page. The author of the story gets to choose a role.

have themselves. Children enjoy the opportunity to take stories off the page and into their classroom.

Developing Critical Thinking Skills

Every time a child evaluates her own ideas, critical thinking is taking place, and because story dictation invites reflection, it helps a child develop critical thinking skills. Each time a child hears her story being read, she has a new opportunity to evaluate her own words. Whenever she asks a teacher to revise her story, perhaps by saying, "No, that's not what I meant," the child is practicing critical thinking.

With older preschoolers, such as five-year-olds, you can invite this kind of reflection by saying, "I'm going to read your story out loud now. Listen and see if I made any mistakes or left anything out." After hearing his story read, a child may realize that there are other ideas or details he wants to include in his story. Acting out a story presents another opportunity for revision. After a story has been performed, you might ask its author, "Is that how you imagined your story would look? Is there anything you'd like to add to make your story better?" Sometimes acting out a story reveals to the storyteller that something is missing.

Here's an example. A four-year-old told this story:

> I saw a movie at my cousin's house. Everybody came. Big brother. Big
> sister. I love my mommy.
> *Matthew, age 4*

After the story had been acted out, the child exclaimed, "That's not how it ends!" When the teacher asked, "How does your story end?" the child replied, "They all go home."

As the whole class watched the teacher write "They all go home" at the bottom of the page, the children learn that a story can be improved when the storyteller has the opportunity to reflect and reconsider.

Reading children's dictated stories aloud or acting them out in a large group also provides opportunities to think about the themes in stories. Sometimes stories challenge children to think about things in new ways. Stories that contain surprises or go against stereotypes present wonderful opportunities for children to develop critical thinking skills.

For example, children frequently tell stories that explore the concepts of good and evil. A storyteller may even label her characters "the good guys" and the "bad guys." When such a story is read aloud or acted out, you can lead a discussion about what makes a good guy good and a bad guy bad. This kind of discussion becomes especially interesting when children dictate stories in which a character turns out to be different from what it first appears to be, like the wolf in this story.

> The princess is in the woods but she saw bunnies. She saw squirrels and a
> wolf. It's a nice wolf. The prince came and held the princess's hand. They
> danced and they got married.
> *Carrie, age 4*

Young children practice critical thinking when they explore how people (and other characters in their stories) don't always do what they're commonly expected to do. In the following children's stories, the bad guys pretend to be good.

> There's two bad guys. One is like a dinosaur and the other is a sword guy.
> They fight good children. The bad guys pretended to be good children.
> That's the end.
> *Danny, age 4*

When you read aloud, act out, or discuss stories like these in a group, children benefit from the challenge of thinking critically about the roles of the characters. In initiating a discussion of Danny's story, you could ask an open-ended question, such as, "If you were in Danny's story, how would you tell the difference between bad guys and good children?" If a child makes a suggestion that reflects rigid or stereotypical thinking, such as "Bad guys always wear dark clothes," reply with a logical, clear example that challenges the child to think more deeply. In this case, you might say, "I'm wearing a dark sweater today. Does that make me a bad guy?" Remember that the purpose of such discussions isn't to teach children right from wrong or how to protect themselves from danger. The purpose is to challenge their thinking about both the characters in their stories and the ideas they may have about the world. As a result of such conversations, the children's stories may become more creative and less predictable.

> Leafler changes to different colors. And he's a bad guy too. He pretends to
> be other people.
> *Robert, age 4*

Another way to challenge children to think critically about stereotypes of good and bad people is to expose them to a diverse variety of stories and picture books. Eugene Trivizas and Helen Oxenbury's *The Three Little Wolves and the Big Bad Pig* is an excellent example of a book that shows children how to see an old story in a new light. (See Appendix C for more read-aloud book recommendations.)

Other interesting questions will naturally arise when children discuss their own stories. Here are three examples of critical thinking questions that were inspired by children's dictated stories: "What makes someone a good friend?" "Is magic real?" and "Is it ever okay to fight?"

The Importance of Reading Aloud to Children

Because stories read aloud to children have tremendous potential to inspire their imagination, enrich their play, and expand their thinking, the books we choose are some of the most important decisions we make regarding curriculum. Each time we read a good storybook aloud to children, we plant the seeds that create a fertile garden in which their own stories can grow and thrive. (For a list of recommended children's books, see Appendix C.)

One way to help children see themselves as authors is to do an author study in your class. For a short period of time, perhaps two weeks, focus on one children's author by reading each day a different book written by that author. Good choices for an author (or author/illustrator) study include Eric Carle, Candace Fleming, Grace Lin, Peggy Rathman, David Shannon, or Mo Willems. Ask the children to compare the authors' books and choose their favorites. Write a class letter to the author. Should you receive a reply, the children will be thrilled and learn that authors are real people.

- Use children's stories and narratives to guide your curriculum planning. Both stories, which are spontaneous and imaginative, and narratives, which are answers to specific teacher-directed questions, can be useful in revealing children's interests and knowledge.

- Remember that acting out children's stories is a great way to create enthusiasm and excitement about telling stories. As stage manager, you are responsible for assigning roles, directing the action, and keeping the stories brief.

- To avoid conflicts, assign roles in random order. Do not allow children to choose who will be in their stories.

- Use stories that contain surprises or stereotypes to start discussions that promote critical thinking. After a story has been read or acted out, ask children how this story differs from others they've heard.

- Read aloud to children throughout the day. Expose children to a wide variety of picture books, folktales, and fairytales.

7

Sharing Stories in the Classroom and with Parents and Families

The way we treat hard copies of the stories children dictate shows children how much we value the written word. When a child finishes dictating a story, do we stuff that page of paper into a folder on a shelf? Or do we create a place of honor for it, where the child and others can read and appreciate the story?

Sharing Stories in the Classroom

Since most stories are only one page long, they can be displayed on a wall or bulletin board at the children's level. The stories on display might be linked to a theme, such as Animal Stories, and paired with children's drawings and artwork related to that theme. Or stories can be part of a bulletin board display that celebrates the storytelling process, perhaps one titled *Our Authors* that includes photos of the children posted next to their stories.

Children feel a sense of pride and affirmation when they see their stories on display. The only downside is not being able to hold and interact with the page after the story is posted on the wall. To remedy this, you can make multiple copies of each story and display a rotating group of stories on the bulletin board while keeping another set of copies for children to use in the classroom.

Classroom copies of stories can be published in booklets or binders. A booklet might consist of a single story spread over several pages, or it might include a series of stories. The books must, of course, be sturdy enough to survive handling by young children. One simple option is to purchase thin binders and plastic sheet protectors in which to place stories. Binders with flexible plastic covers are least expensive, while those with a clear cover allow you to slip a title page into the front of the binder.

This book of stories was made by laminating the covers and binding the pages together with yarn.

Stories in binders can be displayed on the classroom bookshelf along with published books. This practice helps children understand that their stories are similar to the stories they read in books and that authors are real people, just as they are. It also demonstrates that writing words and creating stories is a very powerful act. Just like the other books on the shelf, their own stories can influence and entertain other people.

Stories and Families

Families are often the topic of children's stories. What happens or what might happen in their families is of vital interest to young children and is the source of powerful emotions.

> My daddy bring me to McDonald's. He love me. We buy stuff for everyone.
> My mom give me lunch. A little spider came on my high chair. I love my
> mom. My mom call me sweetie pie.
> *Carrie, age 3*

Since family members play such important roles in children's stories, it only makes sense that those stories are of great interest to parents and other family members. Like anything important that happens to children, the stories they write should be shared with families on a regular basis. Only rarely does a parent feel confused or hurt by something in a child's story. (Such situations are addressed in chapter 13.) Most of the time, parents receive children's stories enthusiastically.

Stories can be shared with families in many informal ways. Stories can be posted on bulletin boards for parents to read when they drop off or pick up their children. Be sure you place the stories on a board that parents pass on their way in and out of the classroom. Stories can be organized around a theme. One titled *Stories about Daddies,* for example, could be posted on the board around Father's Day. Make sure the name of the author of each story is written in big, bold letters so parents can find their child's story easily. Since it may be impossible to include a story from every child every time you post stories, you may want to add a sign that says, MORE STORIES COMING SOON!

Remember that not all parents will notice or take the initiative to read what's posted on a bulletin board. You may need to nudge parents in the right direction: "There's a funny story by Gina posted next to the door. You might want to take a look." You can also store children's journals or a binder of the class's stories on a shelf near the parent sign-in sheet and encourage parents to take a look. And you can make copies of their children's stories and give them to parents to read at home.

Members of a child's extended family also are likely to enjoy that child's stories. Grandparents, for example, often are especially entertained by their grandchildren's stories. If grandparents don't ordinarily have an opportunity to visit the school, extend a special invitation to them to visit and read children's dictated stories. Grandparents who live some distance from their grandchildren may enjoy receiving copies of stories in the mail.

One parent I know posts her son's dictated stories on a family Web page so that extended family members, especially grandparents, can enjoy the stories too. Using computer software can help you offer children's stories to the wider community. If you have access to computers and software, you can post stories on the school's Web site or scan stories and print them in a variety of formats, including publishing them as a regular feature in the school newsletter.

This family uses a Web page to share their son's stories with friends and relatives.

Parents and family members who visit the classroom can play an active role in the creation of stories. Parents can serve as volunteer scribes, not just for their own children but for any child who's interested in dictating a story. This is an especially helpful way to use parent volunteers because it gives parents a clearly defined role. It can be an especially nice way to include fathers in the life of a school.

Story Dictation at Home

Parents often ask what they can do at home to help their child read and write. The first answer, of course, is to read aloud to their child every day. The second answer is to try story dictation at home. Story dictation is a great way for parents to demonstrate to their children the power of reading and writing.

You can begin by giving parents a hand-out describing the basics of story dictation. (In Appendix B, you'll find a sample handout that you can photocopy and give to parents.) Invite families to bring completed stories to school to share with you and the other children. Like stories written at school, stories written at home can be acted out at circle time. Another way to encourage story dictation at home is to designate a special journal for collecting stories, which each family in turn can take home. Ask parents to write down their child's story (or a family story) and then return the journal to school, so the story can be shared with the rest of the class.

Some children really enjoy doing story dictation with their parents at home, but others do not. Like adults, children display a broad range of individual interests, and parents needn't be discouraged if their child is reluctant to dictate stories at home. The child may simply prefer doing other activities with a parent. When one parent I know introduced story dictation to her older child, he wasn't very interested. But when she introduced it to her younger child at around age three, her daughter became passionate about creating stories. That daughter is now seven, and over the years she's created about a hundred stories, many of which she's illustrated and made into storybooks. Although she can write her own words now, she sometimes still dictates stories to her mother. Not every child takes to the story dictation process this easily, as this mother learned from her experience with her son. But sometimes story dictation is just the right thing to draw out a child's creativity and to enhance the bond between parent and child.

As teachers, caregivers, and parents, our role is not only to teach children to read and write but also to create lifelong learners. Of course, not all children who dictate stories are going to become professional writers or storytellers, but most children will go through life seeking meaningful connections with other people. The satisfaction children feel when they share their stories with others creates powerful, positive associations between the written word and feelings of friendship, understanding, and even love. Such positive experiences are what make children avid readers, writers, and learners.

TEACHING TIPS

- Share children's stories with families on a regular basis by posting stories on bulletin boards and sending copies home with families.

- Invite parents to volunteer as scribes in your classroom. At parent meetings, pass around a volunteer scribe sign-up sheet.

- Encourage families to do story dictation at home. (To inform families about story dictation, distribute the handout in Appendix B.)

8

Using Stories for Assessment

Now, more than ever, early childhood educators are being asked to show accountability through various types of formal assessment. There is program assessment, such as the National Association for the Education of Young Children (NAEYC) accreditation process, which measures how well a program meets standards for curriculum, environment, administration, and a variety of other factors. And there is the formal assessment of individual children, which can involve observation and collecting documentation of their learning in portfolios.

Children's dictated stories can be used for both types of assessment. NAEYC accreditation criteria, for example, suggest that children be given "daily opportunities to write and dictate their ideas" (NAEYC 2006). You can use children's dictated stories to demonstrate your program's attainment of this standard. Dictated stories are an authentic source of assessment information when included as documentation in a classroom portfolio or a child's individual portfolio. The stories contain significant information about a child's social-emotional development, language and literacy development, cognitive development, and even physical development.

Experts frequently state that assessment practices must be directly linked to learning standards (Bowman 2006). Currently, early learning standards vary from state to state, so we will use common early childhood curriculum goals, based on NAEYC accreditation criteria, the Head Start Child Outcomes

Framework, and generally accepted developmental milestones to examine how story dictation can be used to evaluate children's growth and progress. We will look at developmental goals in four areas: cognitive development, language and literacy development, social and emotional development, and physical development.

Cognitive Development Goals

During the early childhood years, children generally progress from more concrete to more abstract thinking. They begin to imagine other times and places beyond the here and now as well as points of view different from their own. Children also start to understand the relationship between cause and effect and begin to compare and contrast, which leads to discovering how people and things are the same and different.

Between the ages of three and five, children also start to understand some basic concepts about how the world works. They learn that numbers, tokens (money, for example), and symbols (such as street signs) have a direct relationship to real things and events in the world. They begin to understand that like themselves, other living things have basic needs, that there are forces of nature beyond their control (such as the weather), and that there are things they can do to help them stay safe (for instance, wearing a helmet when riding a bike).

Children also begin to reflect on their own thinking (metacognition) and to understand that they have ideas and can use their minds to solve problems.

We can look for evidence of these goals in children's dictated stories by asking the following questions:

- Is the child creating characters, settings, and actions in her stories that lie beyond her direct experience?
- Is the child incorporating magic into his stories?
- Is the child incorporating ideas from other stories, such as those in books or those told by other children?
- Do actions in the stories demonstrate cause and effect?
- Do the narrator or any of the characters in the story use comparisons to describe people, animals, or objects? For example, does the child use words such as bigger or loudest in her story?

- Do the stories include descriptions of characters traveling from one place to another (showing an understanding of the real or imaginary geography of a setting)?
- Do any of the characters earn or pay with money in the stories?
- Is there any counting in the stories?
- Are numbers used to describe quantities in the stories?
- Do the stories show how people, animals, or other living things have basic needs for nurture, food, water, and shelter?
- Do the stories describe forces of nature, such as storms?
- Do characters in the stories take any action to keep themselves safe or to protect others from harm?
- Does the child talk about what the story is going to be about before dictation begins, showing evidence of planning ahead (metacognition)?
- Does the child ever ask the teacher to revise and improve the story after the words are on the page?
- Does the child discuss the stories after they are written?

Let's look at a child's story that demonstrates some of these milestones of cognitive development.

> Once there was a boy named Nick and he met an alien and the alien had six eyes. And there was a trap with two laser beams and then the trap turned into a cage. But Nick was invulnerable and thick, so he could not get out of the cage. Like Ethan could in the last story. So Ethan walked over from the other story to this story and helped Nick get out. And Nick lives happily ever after. Ethan too.
> *Jack, age 4*

This story demonstrates Jack's abstract thinking and creativity because it features events and creatures that are outside the realm of Jack's direct experience. In this story, we can see how Jack uses his imagination to create a trap that can turn into a cage. Also, Jack is drawing on a number of different sources to create his story, incorporating ideas he's seen on television (laser beams) as well as fairytale language ("happily ever after"). This story, which is an extension of a previous story told by Jack, includes the interesting device of having a character from his previous story, Ethan, walk over to this story to rescue Nick. Jack's use of this device further demonstrates his ability to think abstractly and to make connections between different ideas and sources.

The actions in the story demonstrate an understanding of cause and effect (the alien's trap causes Nick to become stuck in a cage; Ethan's help causes Nick to escape). The mention of the alien's six eyes demonstrates number sense.

Language and Literacy Development Goals

During the early childhood years, children begin to make connections between spoken and written language. Most children begin to understand that letters on a page represent sounds and begin to recognize familiar letters and words. They may also begin to understand the difference between a letter, a word, and a sentence.

Around age three, children also begin to understand that print is permanent and that spoken words can be preserved by writing them down. They may start to notice that writing words takes longer than saying them and that print in the English language progresses from left to right and from top to bottom.

At around age four or five, children begin to recall details from familiar stories and develop the ability to retell a familiar story. They develop the ability to make predictions about what might happen next in a story, and they start to understand that a story has a beginning, a middle, and an end.

During the early childhood years, children steadily build their vocabulary, continually learning and using new words. They often experiment with words and sounds, playing with the rhyme and rhythm of words and language.

We can look for evidence of these goals in children's dicted stories by asking the following questions.

- Does the child watch you write during dictation, following the progress of your pencil with her eyes?
- Does the child ever point to the words on the page or ask questions about what you're writing?
- Does the child recognize or name any of the letters written on the page?
- Does the child recognize his name on the page or any other familiar words?
- Does the child ask to write part of the story herself?
- Does the child slow down his words to match the pace of your writing?

- Does the child seem concerned about whether you're getting the words down correctly?
- Does the child correct you or make revisions when the dictated words are read back?
- Does the child retell or borrow ideas or characters from a story that has been previously read or told to her?
- Does the child tell a story that has a beginning, a middle, and an end?
- Does the child use words in the context of telling a story that he does not usually use in everyday speech?
- Does the child play with words—for example, by using rhymes, repetition, or alliteration?

Let's look at the following story and see what we can learn about this child's language and literacy development.

A Thanksgiving Poem

Hunters are coming!

I like hunters.

They give us lots and lots of good food.

And lots and lots and lots of terrible stuff.

Thanksgiving turkeys too.

Turkey turkey turkey!

Heidi, age 4

In this poem, Heidi is both playing with language and exploring a variety of concepts related to hunting and eating. Heidi came up with the idea of titling her dictation "A Thanksgiving Poem" without any prompting from a teacher. This piece of dictation demonstrates that Heidi has some understanding of the literary conventions of poetry, such as incomplete sentences and repetition ("Turkey turkey turkey!"). She also knows that some forms of writing, such as poems, usually have a title, and she knows that the title announces what is to follow. During the dictation process, Heidi directed the arrangement of words on the page, with only a few words on each line, so that it would look like a poem. With serious concentration, she watched the adult write her words and insisted that the adult read the completed poem aloud and point to each word as it was read. Heidi is developing her own voice as a writer and poet, capturing the

Some older preschoolers and some kindergarteners will make attempts to write their own stories, using invented spelling.

reader's attention in the first line of her poem with the exciting announcement "Hunters are coming!" She has also created an interesting contrast by stating that the hunters bring both "good food" and "terrible stuff."

Social and Emotional Development Goals

During the early childhood years, children begin to find new ways to express and describe their own feelings. Gradually, they also begin to recognize and understand the feelings of others.

Children can form trusting relationships with their teachers and other caring adults as early as infancy, and these relationships continue to develop through the preschool years. Around the age of three or four, children begin to form friendships with other children. They begin to play and work in partnership with each other, and they start to develop strategies for resolving conflicts without force.

Depending on what emotions and behaviors are valued in their family and culture, children may develop autonomy and independence. At the same time, they also develop the ability to be helpful to others and to function as supportive members of a group.

Around the age of four or five, children start to develop a stronger self-identity and begin to understand and empathize with people from diverse backgrounds.

We can look for evidence of these goals in children's dictated stories by asking questions such as these:

- Does the child mention or describe the emotions of characters in his story?
- Does the child's story describe a friendship or other trusting relationship?
- Does the story describe a fear or hope?
- Does the story describe a fear or hope that is resolved over the course of the story?
- Does the story describe a problem?
- Does the story describe a solution to a problem?
- Does the story describe the child's family?
- Are any of the stories written in the first person?
- Did the author of the story collaborate with other children during the dictation process? Did she consider and incorporate the ideas of others into her story?

- Did the author of the story volunteer to have the story read to or acted out with the other children?
- If so, did the child exhibit a sense of pride, through posture or facial expressions, when the story was read or performed?

As we look at the following story, let's see what social and emotional milestones we can identify through it.

> The kitty went for a walk. Lily petted her. She liked that. She licked Lily. It felt good.
>
> *Lily, age 3*

Lily's simple story describes a positive encounter between a kitty and a child. Lily includes two sentences that describe the quality of the encounter: "She liked that" and "It felt good." This story shows that Lily can understand and express positive, caring emotions. Because Lily pets the cat and the cat licks Lily, the story also suggests that Lily understands the reciprocal, give-and-take nature of positive relationships. When this story was later acted out by Lily and the other children, Lily's smiles and obvious excitement demonstrated her pleasure in sharing her story with her friends.

Physical Development Goals

Between the ages of three and five, children continue to refine their fine-motor skills. They usually learn to grasp a pencil or crayon, and they begin to draw lines, shapes, and figures. They also may make lines that imitate the writing of letters and words. They may even begin to write letters. Children are also developing gross-motor skills, which demonstrate their increasing coordination and skills, such as jumping, hopping, and balancing on one foot.

We can look for evidence of these goals in the way children illustrate, label, and make beginning attempts at writing their own stories:

- Does the child draw pictures to go with a story?
- Does the child make lines that imitate writing?
- Does the child attempt to form actual letters?
- Does the child write his or her own name?
- When acting out stories, is the child able to move with coordination and purposefully avoid bumping into other children or falling over?

P

My story begins with Snow White.
Snow White I'm going to do today.
The Wicked old witch turns into
a hag. Then she tries to move
a big rock and tried to and crush the dwarves
and she caught her balance and
fell to her doom. And then
the poor dwarves made a little
glass for poors Snow White.
And she wanted to stay with
them and one day a prince
I came and took her on the
horse and they lived happily
ever after in a castle and then
they got married. And they lived
happily ever after.

We see here examples of the child's controlled scribbling, along with her beginning attempts to add her own story to the one she's dictated. When this story was acted out with the group, the children also demonstrated gross-motor skills by hopping and rolling on the rug.

Using Story Dictation for Assessment

As illustrated in the above examples, a great variety of valuable and authentic assessment information can be gathered from children's dictated stories. The three to five minutes spent taking dictation from a child may result in a story that can be used to meet a variety of assessment mandates. In a Head Start classroom, information from dictated stories can be used to complete the Preschool Child Observation Record (COR). If you use portfolios to document children's learning, the stories can be included in the portfolio along with a description of the developmental abilities that can be demonstrated from the story. Finally, in settings in which an emergent curriculum or a project approach is used, children's stories also can become an important part of classroom documentation.

Sharing Assessment Information with Families

One of the most important reasons we do assessment is to share information about children's growth with parents and families. Sharing dictated stories with parents is an excellent way to demonstrate how much their children are learning. That's why reading and discussing a few recently dictated stories is a great way to begin a parent-teacher conference. Parents enjoy the humor of the stories and often are amazed by the creativity expressed by their own children. Sharing the stories also communicates to parents that their child's teacher truly cares about and is interested in how their child is thinking and learning.

Regardless of how you collect or publish the stories, at some point you should collect each child's stories in chronological order in a single binder. Depending on how you display or share the stories with families, you may need to make photocopies of them. It's well worth the trouble. When a child makes the transition to kindergarten, you can read the stories together to help the child see his own growth and feel confident in his own ability to learn. A binder of a child's stories also makes a wonderful good-bye gift for families that they'll cherish like no other.

TEACHING TIPS

● Save copies of children's dictated stories. Be sure to date each one so you can use them to document a child's progress over a period of time.

● Use the questions in this chapter or another assessment tool to target specific skills that are demonstrated in each story.

● When conducting parent conferences, you might begin the conversation by sharing one of the child's dictated stories. Even if the parents have read the story before, they'll enjoy hearing you, the teacher, praise it and talk about the many different skills that are demonstrated in their child's story.

PART 3

Interpreting Children's Stories

Children's dictated stories are fascinating to read, because they invite us to think deeply about the individual child who told the story, about patterns of child development, and perhaps even about our own work. It is this kind of reflection that is so essential to our professional growth.

This part of the book is a guide for that reflection. The chapters that follow offer guidance for understanding the meaning behind children's stories and the context in which the stories were written. Chapter 9 presents some basic strategies for interpreting children's dictated stories and looks at some common story themes. In chapter 10, we look at how children use humor in stories, and in chapter 11, we consider the conflict their stories often contain. Chapter 12 looks at how gender and culture influence the way children tell and receive stories. Finally, chapter 13 offers assistance to teachers and caregivers who have concerns about a child's story, perhaps because the story contains conflict, violence, or another element that makes them feel uncomfortable.

The most important idea to keep in mind throughout these discussions is the power of reflection. When teachers and caregivers reflect upon children's work through careful thought and observation, through consultation and supervision, and through time and patience, everyone grows and learns.

9

Searching for Meaning

Sometimes a child tells a story that is so odd, or funny, or beautiful, it takes your breath away. You can't help but wonder how the child thought of it and what the story means. In this chapter, we'll learn some strategies for reflecting on the meaning behind a child's dictated story. We'll also discuss how the meaning of a child's story is related to the context in which it was written. Finally, we'll look at the meaning behind some of the most basic types of stories children tell, including stories based on illustrations, stories that are retellings of familiar storybooks, and stories about families.

Stories in Context

Here's an example of a child's dictated story that I find especially unique and interesting.

> Once upon a time there was a dolly and her children died. And she went to the store and bought garlic bread and the little green bits reminded her of her dead children. She stuffed it all in her mouth at once and chewed it up into tiny bits. Then she wished that her children would come alive again. She had a big stick and she banged the wind chimes like this: "Ding!" She wished for the good fairies to come and Poof! Her children were alive again. She

was so happy that she gave them a kiss and a gift and they lived happily
ever after.

Robin, age 5

I've never met the child who told this story. A copy of it was given to me by
her teacher. When I read the story, I was amazed by the unusual imagery. I was
especially curious about those little green bits (perhaps oregano?) in the garlic
bread that reminded the dolly of her dead children. What would cause a child
to tell a story like this? What does the story mean? Can children's stories, like
dreams, be interpreted by assigning meaning to specific symbols?

Unlike dreaming, the storytelling process is a conscious act that can be
influenced by a number of factors, including stories the child has heard, who
the child's friends and family are, and the television shows and movies the child
has seen. A story may even be inspired by items the child can see while dictating
the story. To explore the meaning behind children's stories, you need to ask what
factors influenced the telling of a child's story, why the themes in the story may
appeal to that child, and what other information you may have about the child's
interests and experiences that might have shaped the story.

Scissors. You cut yourself.

The marker. You can mark yourself.

A knife. You can cut yourself.

A puncher. You can cut yourself.

The end.

José, age 3

I happen to know that José told this story about some of the items he could
see in his classroom while he was telling his story. (That knife was a plastic toy.)
Since the origins of the story appear to be obvious and straightforward, how are
we to interpret the meaning behind José's story? Its recurring image seems to be
of someone getting cut, so we can ask ourselves why this theme may interest this
child. Perhaps José is using his story to express some of his fears, such as the fear
of getting hurt or the fear of an unfamiliar environment.

Unless we know something about José and the larger circumstances under
which this story was written, it's almost impossible to guess its meaning. This
is true of just about any child's story. Since I do not personally know José, or
Robin, the author of the garlic bread story, I can only guess about the meanings

of their stories. If I knew these children and something about their experiences at the time their stories were written, I might be able to form some ideas about why José seemed to be so focused on the possibilities of danger and why the little green bits reminded the dolly in Robin's story of her dead children.

As a contrast, let's consider a story told by a child I know well.

> It's about Sleeping Beauty's dress and long hair, curly long hair and pink and red dress and beautiful flower socks and beautiful flower shoes. The Rescue Heroes drop Sleeping Beauty into the ice cream cake. She gots really freezed and she doesn't move any time. She dies when she's in the ice.
> *Sean, age 4*

At first glance, this story appears to be about powerful figures (Rescue Heroes) getting rid of Sleeping Beauty. Since the storyteller is a boy, it's easy to assume that he dislikes princesses like Sleeping Beauty and identifies with the Rescue Heroes. Perhaps this is just another of the many stories boys commonly tell about superheroes and their powers. But I happen to know that Sean was recently teased by his older brothers because he enjoys playing with dolls. With that bit of knowledge, let's look at the story again.

Notice how lovingly Sean describes Sleeping Beauty's hair and clothes. She has "long hair, curly long hair," and she wears "beautiful flower socks and beautiful flower shoes." Perhaps the character Sean most identifies with is Sleeping Beauty. Perhaps the Rescue Heroes are like Sean's brothers. Just as the brothers interrupted Sean's play with their teasing, the Rescue Heroes put an end to Sleeping Beauty. Though we can't know for sure, we can make the educated guess that Sean's story is related to his attempts to make sense of the conflict between his enjoyment of playing with dolls and his brothers' teasing. With just this bit of information about Sean, my understanding of his story becomes so much richer. And knowing what I know, I can look for opportunities to give Sean support as he works through this conflict.

Knowing something about the author of the story and the context in which it was written is essential, but there are also some broad and common categories into which we can sort children's stories. Regardless of geography and circumstances, most children's stories share a few similar themes. Families, monsters, superheroes, and animals are frequent topics of children's stories, and we'll examine these topics in detail in the next few chapters. But let's begin with the kinds of stories that are most concrete—the stories children tell about drawings they've made.

Stories Based on Illustrations

A child draws a picture with markers or crayons, and the teacher or child care provider says, "Tell me about your picture." She writes the child's words at the bottom of the picture, and a story is born. Stories based on illustrations are important because the drawing process, combined with the writing models the child observes, help the child make the transition from random scribbles to controlled drawing to writing letters and words. Although such stories often are also a child's first experience with dictation, many children continue to enjoy drawing illustrations for stories even after they can write words and sentences on their own.

Children may be inspired to dictate a story from a drawing they've made.

This child first created a drawing and then dictated words to her teacher to describe it. The teacher documented not only the child's words but also what question had been asked to elicit the child's response.

Sometimes there isn't a lot of meaning to these stories beyond the child's desire to describe what he or she sees on the page.

> Here's the red. Here's the blue.
>
> *Maggie, age 2 (describing her drawing)*

Preschool-age children usually are not developmentally capable of creating drawings that are as complex and varied as the stories in their heads. Often, but not always, a dictated story based upon a drawing will be limited to what the child is able to represent on a two-dimensional piece of paper.

> I make a house and I made a chair so I can sit down. I put my name. I can
> go in my house and I can open a window. I am going up, me and Mommy.
> I no want to sit there anymore. The end.
>
> *Mark, age 3 (describing his drawing)*

There are always exceptions, of course. Sometimes a child's drawing and dictated words can suggest a meaning beyond a literal interpretation of the image. One striking example of this is a page from a three-year-old child's journal created only a week after her mother died of cancer. The child drew just two circles, side by side, one large, one smaller. Then she dictated these words:

> Monster. This is a tunnel. A person is in there.

We can make an educated guess that the monster and the tunnel represent the grief and fear this child is experiencing.

Retelling Stories from Books

Another common occurrence in children's storytelling is the retelling of stories from a book, particularly fairytales. Sometimes the story has no significant meaning to the child, especially if he has been directed to retell a story selected by a teacher or care provider. Here's an example of a story a child wrote after her teacher suggested she retell the story *Stone Soup,* which had been read to the class earlier in the day. We can see that the child has accurately described specific details from the original story.

> Some soldiers come. And then he say, "Everybody make the stone soup."
> And everybody eat it up and then they sleep. They just put water on the fire
> and then morning was coming. Then it was time to go and the soldier went
> home and everybody was going home.
> *Bonnie, age 3*

The retelling of a story from a book becomes more interesting when the child initiates the telling. Then we can wonder what it is about that particular story that has captured the child's interest. It's also interesting to note the ways a child might change a story and add his own ideas.

Here's a child's retelling of the story *Jack and the Beanstalk.*

> Jack and his friends went up a beanstalk and they saw a giant. The giant
> came running after them. The giant grabbed him and put him towards his
> mouth. He put Jack and his friends in his mouth. And the giant put his hand
> in his mouth and took Jack and his friend out of his mouth. And the giant

gave Jack and his friend to his doggie to eat for dinner. The doggie ate Jack for dinner. Jack's friends are named Tony and Dina. And the doggie ate Tony for breakfast. The doggie's name is Jessica. So Tony and Dina went down the beanstalk. And Jessica, the doggie, was nice to Tony and Dorian.

Renee, age 4

To explore why this story may hold meaning for this child, we can look at the ways her story differs from the original tale. For example, in Renee's story, the danger of getting gobbled up seems to be the primary focus of attention. There's no mention of magic beans, no fee-fi-fo-fumming. The key question is who's going to be eaten and by whom. Renee also seems to be playing with the concepts of danger and escape. Jack and his friends get put in the giant's mouth, and then are miraculously taken out again. Tony gets eaten for breakfast but later reappears unharmed and goes down the beanstalk. Finally, Renee has chosen to introduce additional characters to the story. Poor Jack is eaten by the giant's dog, and it's Tony and Dina who somehow come out on top.

Using this information, along with some observations of Renee's play, we can make some educated guesses about the meaning behind her story. Renee is at a phase in her development when she's very concerned about making and having friends. During play, she competes for the attention of a few favorite friends and becomes upset if she doesn't have someone to play with or a friend to sit with. In light of these observations, it's possible that Renee's story reflects some of her anxieties about having friends. There is a sense of competition between the characters in her story: Who will be saved? Who will get eaten? Perhaps the tension in the story parallels Renee's tension about friendships: Who'll be chosen to play? Who'll be left out?

Renee's story, which at first appears to be a simple retelling of a familiar tale, may be a reflection of her deepest hopes and fears. Of course, this interpretation of Renee's story is simply an educated guess based on several observations of her pretend play. And as I've mentioned before, we can never be completely certain of the meaning behind a child's story. But her story can be one clue, among others, suggesting that this issue concerns Renee, and suspecting this offers us an opportunity to follow up in our observations and support of her social-emotional development.

Stories about Families

When children choose their own topics for stories, by far the most popular topic is their family.

> Mommy.
> Daddy.
> Julietta.
> Luis.
> In the house. The happy house.
> *Luis, age 3*

It only makes sense that family is the most important subject in the stories of young children, whose strongest emotional attachments are to parents and family members. Vivian Gussin Paley has said that there is something holy about the stories children tell about their parents (1990). This is especially true of the stories told by children in full-day programs, who are separated from their parents during the long workday. Telling stories about their parents is one way children can feel closer to their families while they're apart. Stories can be a way of holding on to happy memories and revisiting pleasurable moments.

> Me and my mommy. My mommy took me and my cousin to the video
> store. We rented a movie.
> *Anton, age 4*

It's also not surprising that food often plays an important role in happy family stories.

> I ate chicken with my daddy. We had juice and ice cream and cheese pops.
> *Cole, age 3*

Telling a story also is a way for a child to express hopes and desires related to parents and families.

> When my birthday comes my mommy will take me to a water park. I'll go
> down the slide a hundred times.
> *Alena, age 4*

There is much that goes on within families that young children do not understand. Sometimes telling a story is a way a child can try to make sense of a confusing situation.

> Mommy goes to the hospital. The angel gave them the baby. She put it in a blanket and took it home.
> *David, age 3*

When a child tells a story about his family, that story often becomes a source of comfort to the child, rather like a familiar blanket or teddy bear. I once worked with a child who found so much comfort in the stories she dictated about her mommy that we kept a folded copy of one of her stories under her pillow during naptime.

Mass Media Characters

It's not surprising that characters from movies, books, television, cereal boxes, and advertisements also pop up in children's stories. These pervasive and profitable characters, from Spider-Man to Polly Pocket, aren't likely to go away soon, and children can't help but be influenced by them.

> This is about Sleeping Beauty. She had a dog and it was nice. And she married the prince. The girl, Sleeping Beauty, died. The prince had to get a new wand to save the girl. Then Sleeping Beauty was alive and she had a pink dress. It had purple and brown and purple and blue dots on her dress. Her mom told the brother and sister they could go on the computer. They really wanted to and they got on Disney.com. And they wanted to go to Neopets on the computer.
> *Naomi, age 4*

The first reason why children may tell stories about mass media characters is that it's so easy to do. Because children are likely to be exposed to such characters through all the media that saturate our everyday life, these characters may be the first images that come to their minds. The familiarity of these characters can be comforting to children.

> Shrek and Princess Fiona go to Shrek's house. The donkey is in the house. He's silly. Puss 'n Boots is cool. He put his claws on Shrek Two's pants. Everybody sings a song at the end. .
> *Allin, age 4*

Second, children use these stories to connect to each other, since they often know the same characters. Oftentimes, the influence of the popular mass media can be seen first in children's pretend play.

> Me and Zachary go outside and play Spider-Man. And me and Anton play
> Power Rangers and Spider-Man.
> *Steve, age 4*

If another child wants to join in a group of children who are playing Spider-Man, there's no need to explain to the new child what they're doing. Any child who's seen Spider-Man on television or in a movie can easily join in the play. These familiar characters serve a similar function in children's stories. For example, a child can tell the story.

> Power Rangers. Pow!

and most of the children who hear it will easily understand and relate to it. If the story is acted out, many children will be eager to play the roles of these popular characters.

Sometimes a child chooses to tell a story about a popular character because he or she strongly identifies with the character. For example, a Spanish-speaking child may love Dora the Explorer because Dora speaks Spanish. Or perhaps the character represents something the child desires, such as Spider-Man's power, Sleeping Beauty's good fortune, or Scooby Doo's friends.

> Once upon a time there was Scooby and he had friends. They were dog
> friends. They were nice dogs.
> *Sandra, age 4*

There is nothing inherently wrong with children dictating stories about mass media characters. Telling stories about popular characters often gives children great pleasure, which may encourage them to dictate more stories and to associate positive emotions with storytelling activities. Furthermore, every story dictation experience, regardless of the topic, helps children develop their storytelling and language skills. But after children have had some experience telling stories and you think they're ready for new challenges, they can and should be encouraged to expand their repertoire of story characters. You can do this directly, by gently encouraging children to create variations on their favorite characters. For example, if a child often tells stories about Cinderella, you might say, "I wonder if you might be able to make up your own princess today. Use your own imagination. What does your own princess wear? What is her name? What special powers does she have?" Another way to help children expand upon a narrow cast of characters is to read aloud to them from a rich variety of children's storybooks. (For picture book ideas, see Appendix C.) Regular exposure to a variety of powerful heroes, elegant princesses, and clever animals helps children become better storytellers.

Imitation and Stories

When young children imitate each other's stories, which they do frequently, they aren't just copying; they're also collaborating. The old expression "Imitation is the sincerest form of flattery" applies here. When two children tell stories with similar actions, characters, or wording, it shows they're paying attention to each other. What's more, the imitating child may add details that provide the storyline with a new twist, thereby demonstrating his own critical thinking about the subject. In the following stories, two boys each tell about the construction of a house. After hearing Alex's story, Carl chooses to tell his own.

Alex's Construction Story

The workers put the doors in and then they put some wooden stairs in for some other stairs. And then they put up some bricks and then they dig stuff with the dump trucks. Then they put boards on the stairs that weren't done yet.

Alex, age 5

Carl's Construction Story

The crane picked up some bricks and put them down. Then he carried some more and made the doors and windows. Then the wood got close to some more. Then the people needed to climb up some stairs. Then the crane dropped some sticks down.

Carl, age 5

The stories are similar in that both imagine vividly the construction of a house and include details about materials and the use of equipment. But each boy focuses on slightly different details, making the story his own.

Repeating Stories

Sometimes a child tells the same stories with the same characters over and over again, especially when the characters are popular in the mass media. As a teacher or child care provider, you can help children become more creative storytellers by engaging them in open-ended conversations about their stories. Such conversations will help you learn more about the meaning of the stories for this child and help the child think more deeply about the stories. You might begin a conversation by saying, for example, "I've noticed that the stories you tell are usually about Power Rangers killing a snake monster. I'd like to learn more about this story." Then ask the child some open-ended questions about the story. Challenging a child to think about what happened to the characters before the story started and after the story ends may take the child in a new direction. For example, you might ask, "Where did the snake monster come from?" or "What did the Power Rangers do after they killed the snake monster?" As a result of this kind of discussion, the child may begin expanding upon her stories and developing new storylines and characters.

Another way to help children expand the cast of characters in their stories is to introduce them to new and challenging children's books and a rich assortment of fairytales and folktales. (A list of suggested titles appears in Appendix C.) By showing children a wide variety of ways to represent their ideas, we often can jump-start a child who's stuck telling stories with stock characters.

If a child persists in telling the same story, be patient and allow him to continue to tell the story he wants to tell. When a child repeats a story, it's usually because that story is serving an important function for the child. Perhaps the predictability of the story offers the child security and comfort. Perhaps the story is helping the child work through a confusing or difficult experience, such as getting hurt on the playground, as the story that follows suggests. Allowed continuing opportunity to tell that story, the child may be able to bring it to a happy conclusion and eventually move on to new stories.

> You get hurt on the swings. And your friends can play with you. And your friends go to the park with you. Your friends go to your house. And your friends go home. And your friends say bye-bye to you.
> *Danielle, age 4*

TEACHING TIPS

- When reflecting on the meaning of a child's story, always consider the context in which the story was dictated. What was going on in the child's life at the time the story was told?

- Beware of placing too much importance on interpreting the meaning behind children's stories. Our interpretations are simply guesses, not sureties.

- Remember that a good way for a child to gain some first experiences dictating words to an adult is to have her dictate stories based on her drawings. Don't be surprised, however, if the child uses very concrete language, such as simple descriptions of the colors and shapes on the page.

- Encourage children to retell familiar stories (for example, *The Three Little Pigs)* that will give them experience dictating with storylines they already know well.

- If a child is having a hard time coming up with an idea for a story, suggest a story about the child's family. Say, "Tell me a story about your family" or "Tell me a story about something you'd like to do with your mommy or daddy."

- Use story time or circle time to expose children to a wide variety of excellent picture books. Folktales and fairytales about animals work well with preschoolers. Consider the African folktale about Anansi the spider or the European fairytale *Goldilocks and the Three Bears.* (See Appendix C for additional recommended picture books.)

10 Funny Stories

> One day there was a pretty ball, but Buster came and found it and she was
> a lady but his nickname was Candyeater and his last name was Tigershoe.
> *Julian, age 4 (laughing as he speaks)*

Children often tell silly stories that make them or others laugh. Although it may appear that such stories are purely for entertainment, what they allow is an opportunity for children to explore language in new and interesting ways.

As most child care providers can attest, what a three- to five-year-old child finds funny is very different from what is funny to an adult. Children often are amused by stories that involve bathroom humor or name-calling or that are just wildly silly. On the other hand, when an adult finds a young child's story amusing, it's often because the child has made a charming mistake in the use of language, perhaps by using an idiom or expression in an unusual way.

> Goldilocks eats the porridge all up! And the bears see there's no more.
> The bears kick her out. They say, "Good-bye! Stay away until the cows
> come home!"
> *Brooke, age 4*

> My monster trucks are a little cheap. That means they're broken.
> *James, age 5*

They were so hungry, they ate their mac and cheese like a twinkle in the sky.
Heidi, age 5

When the humor is unintentional and the child is unaware of the odd way she's used language, we must take care not to hurt the child's feelings by openly laughing at the story. But we certainly can take pleasure in such charming stories after the children have gone home.

Language Play

One time there was a little boy. And his name was "Harry is my little Potter."
Sam, age 4

The sense of humor typically displayed by three- to five-year-old children is not very sophisticated. Children often find humor simply through playing with words in nonsensical ways, as the example above shows.

The next story incorporates another kind of nonsense young children enjoy.

The space guy shoot the fireworks. Then he shoot macaroni noodles. The noodles slipped across the sky. The aliens fell down. "Help! The noodles are slipping us!"
Logan, age 4

In his story, Logan has used silly words (who can resist smiling when they say "noodle"?), and he has used them to create a silly image (the aliens falling down on slippery noodles). Both kinds of silliness are wonderful ways for children to play with language, ways that should be encouraged.

Potty Talk

Bathroom humor provides an endless source of enjoyment for preschoolers, so children are bound to incorporate it into their stories.

Once upon a time Snow White peed on herself. Her mother said, "Go change!" She didn't put no clothes on. Everybody could see her booty.
Lily, age 3

Although many teachers and child care providers don't allow children to use words like booty in regular conversations, some of us are more tolerant of this kind of humor in a dictated story, because we accept that when children are free to express themselves, more creativity and learning take place. My suggestion is to allow children to tell such stories freely at the writing table but to put restrictions on sharing them with the group. I wouldn't, for example, read this story aloud at circle time or invite children to act it out.

There are two reasons why it's important that young children have a safe place to tell "potty talk" stories. First, such experiences encourage children to try using language in new ways, which helps build language skills. Second, for many children, potty talk is the only way they feel comfortable expressing their growing knowledge about their bodies and how they work. Told one-on-one or in a very small group, a potty talk story like Lily's could spark a discussion in which you might be able to help children resolve misconceptions or fears they have about their bodies.

The Birds make the poop at my house.

Some children are likely to be amused by this drawing and its dictated words, which refer to birds "pooping" on houses.

If a child tells a story that contains potty talk and wants it to be shared with the group, I would explain to her that the story has to be changed before it can be shared. I would point out which words and phrases are "words we usually say in private" or, if you know this to be true, "words that your family does not like you to use." Then give the child a choice: "We can leave your story like this and put it aside for now. Or, if you like, we can change some of the words so the story will be ready for sharing with others. Which would you like to do?" Usually the child will agree to make the changes and present a suitable story to the group.

Trash Talking

Another kind of humor that young children really enjoy but teachers and child care providers sometimes disapprove of is called trash talking. It occurs when characters in a story insult each other or say something especially negative.

Under no circumstances should children be allowed to insult each other within the context of their stories. Insults are hurtful enough for adults. In a child's world, they not only cause personal pain but also can diminish a child's sense of trust and safety in a setting. Suppose a child dictates a story in which another child in the group is insulted or hurt.

> The magic turned Martin into a little yucky bug. Then a foot stepped on the bug.
> *Ricky, age 4*

Martin is likely to feel not only hurt by these words but also threatened. To prevent this kind of situation, story dictation is sometimes practiced under rules saying that you can't tell a story about someone else in the class unless you have his permission, or you can't say anything mean in a story about someone else in the class.

It is unnecessary to set up such rules when you first begin story dictation in your class or family child care setting. These kinds of situations arise naturally, and they create teachable moments that offer excellent opportunities for discussion. Invite the children to be part of the problem solving and decision making. By carefully protecting the identity of the storytellers and their subjects, you can initiate and facilitate these discussions in ways that do not embarrass or blame children. For example, you might say, "Today someone told a story about another child in our class. In the story, that other child gets hurt. I'm wondering if that's okay. What do you all think? Is it okay for a storyteller to tell a story in which someone real, someone from our own class, gets hurt?" Don't feel pressured to resolve the problem and set a rule right away. Show the children that important decisions take time and careful consideration. In the meantime, be sure to set aside any questionable stories. Once the problem has been resolved, and if a rule has been made, you can revisit those stories with their authors and decide together whether or not their stories need to be changed.

In almost everything we do, we must balance the need to allow children freedom to explore with the need to provide guidance and structure. There is always some give and take between these two demands, and that is true with story dictation. But if we give children some freedom to experiment with their stories, they're more likely to develop into creative storytellers. Here's a case in point, a story that was told by a five-year-old child who had several years of experience in dictating stories to her teacher. Her creative use of humor and improvisation rivals that of many adult authors.

> Once upon a time there was a princess that got confused all the time. And her father, the king, thought that she did it for fun. And he sent her to her room. And she jumped out the window.
>
> The king got so mad that he made her sleep in the dungeon for one night. And next morning he said to himself, "What has gotten into that girl?" Then he said, "What is wrong with you?" to the princess.
>
> On her third birthday the king said, "Maybe I should get you a copy of a book called *Never Forget Things* and that will teach you not to forget." But she kept on forgetting even though he got her the book.
>
> One day she said, "Maybe we should go fishing," but she caught no fish and the king caught four fish. And the princess could do beautiful embroidery but she couldn't fish.
>
> She found a prince and they married and the princess never forgetted again. They went camping and they had a good time. They went swimming with their beach ball. They found a robin's nest with eggs in it. They saw a shooting star at night.
> The end.
> *Carla, age 5*

TEACHING TIPS

- Be careful not to laugh at a child who tells a story by using language in an unusual or surprising way. Instead, take time later on to share and enjoy the unintentional humor in these stories with other adults.

- When they dictate their stories, allow children to experiment with language and ideas—including potty talk and trash talking, as long as the trash talking isn't directed at another child. Having this freedom will help them gain confidence and new skills using words. Recognize that you probably won't want to allow stories with potty talk or trash talking to be shared with the group.

- Invite the children to help you make rules about what kinds of stories can or cannot be shared with the group, especially stories told about each other. Their sensitivity and insights may surprise you.

11 Stories about Conflict

Children's stories often contain a great deal of conflict, frequently mirroring their pretend play. The conflict may take the form of two superheroes fighting, or it may be more subtle, as in a story about a lost princess. I've observed that children's stories about conflict usually fall into three categories: monster stories, superhero stories, and what I call "happy kitty" stories. In monster stories and superhero stories, the conflict usually takes center stage. Happy kitty stories, on the other hand, describe fanciful or domestic scenes with only minor tension or conflict. In these stories, which are often inhabited by animals or princesses, the characters play together, care for each other, and often eat their favorite foods. Although the conflict in these stories is often less obvious, it is still significant. In the light of our knowledge about individual children, we can discover, as we notice these themes emerge, a great deal about the interests and desires that fuel each child's stories.

Monsters, Giants, and Sharks

Monsters are a frequent theme in children's stories. Such stories are usually scary and describe very dangerous situations. Sometimes another creature—a giant, a ghost, a shark, a vampire, an alligator—takes the place of the monster, but the content of the stories is very much the same: a monster comes and does something terrible. Frequently the story ends without any positive resolution.

Monster! In the cubby. Go away! No more!
Anthony, age 4

Monster stories can also be very violent and chaotic.

Once upon a time there was like crashing walls. And then they were knocking all of the cats out of the house. The scissors broke the whole house up. And a giant came and knocked all the people out. When the people came out, a baby was not walking, but was crawling. The baby scared all the people. And they went around the house. The end.
Kim, age 4

The fact that children tell monster stories so frequently and in so many different circumstances tells us that these stories must fulfill some universal need. Asked to "tell me a monster story," most young children will respond with passion and enthusiasm, waving their arms about as they speak. In her book *Teacher,* Sylvia Ashton-Warner describes teaching Maori children to read by allowing them to dictate to her the words they found most interesting and meaningful. She discovered that many of the words the children were most interested in learning were words related to fear, words including *ghost, wild, police, spider, kill, knife, hit, fight, thunder, alligator,* and *cry.* Ashton-Warner called such words "one look" words because the children were so intensely interested in their meaning that they learned to read them after just one look (1963, pp. 44–45).

Having occasional feelings of fear is quite normal for young children. Fears that most children experience from time to time include fear of the dark, fear of things that cause loud noises (such as a barking dog or a police siren), fear of thunder and lightning, and, of course, fear of monsters. These fears usually begin around the time children are developing the ability to think abstractly, generally between ages three and five. Although children at this age are beginning to have the ability to imagine a world beyond their immediate experience, they do not yet have the knowledge and experience to clearly understand the difference between what is real and what is imaginary. It is also normal for young children to occasionally feel deeper fears, fears that they may not be able to put into words, such as fear of separation from their parents or fear of change.

You may notice that during times of stress and change, children seem more fearful of monsters, the dark, or storms. In their storytelling, this may be represented by dictating more stories about monsters. Dictating such stories may be one way children try to express their deeper fears, because monsters can become symbols for fears that may be too difficult to talk about or fears about things a child may not fully understand. Telling frightening stories allows children to face their fears safely, because when they tell a story, they are in control of what happens.

For this very reason, children often tell monster stories in the third person. Understandably reluctant to place themselves in a monster story, children speak in the third person to maintain some control over what happens. The content of a monster story may be so frightening to them that they must distance themselves by telling the story in a way that makes clear this is happening to someone else. Telling the story in third person also demonstrates children's ability, even if it's only intuitively, to understand the significance of a story's point of view.

> The monster tried to catch the dogs and suddenly it got dark out. The dogs
> ran faster and faster. And they went in the monster's cave. They got caught
> by the monster. The monster's throat was way big. It ate the doggies and
> took them off its breath.
> *Sonya, age 4*

Sometimes, however, a child is brave enough to tell a story in the first person.

> Once upon a time, a monster got me. He threw me into his mouth. He
> sawed me into a saw. The end.
> *Kevin, age 4*

It can be therapeutic and emotionally affirming for children to feel mastery over their feelings during times of stress or fear.

Resolution in Monster Stories

As mentioned above, monster stories often have no resolution.

> An alligator, a fish, and a shark. A elephant swim with the shark. Elephant
> swim with alligator. The crocodile touch the sky. He eat the children. They
> in his mouth. The end.
> *Chris, age 3*

It can be disconcerting to adults when a story like Chris's ends without resolution. We might be tempted to suggest an ending: "Maybe the children jumped out of the crocodile's mouth and swam away?" Wanting children to feel safe, we may try to protect them from whatever stirred up such stories. It is important to resist the temptation to help a child end a story. We must remember that these stories serve an important function for children by allowing them to express an uncomfortable emotion. As receptive, listening adults, we should simply mirror the child's feelings: "That's quite a scary story, isn't it?"

In most cases, monster stories are normal expressions of childhood fears. On rare occasions, however, a child's monster story can cause the teacher or child care provider to feel upset because the story is especially violent or the fear expressed by the child seems unusual or extreme. (Responding to disturbing stories is discussed in detail in chapter 13.)

Superheroes and Happy Kitties

Superhero stories describe powerful characters with superhuman abilities, whereas happy kitty stories feature friendly animals and attractive princesses who experience milder conflict. Unlike monster stories, superhero stories and happy kitty stories usually end with the conflict being resolved. Although superhero stories tend to be told by boys and happy kitty stories by girls, these stories share an important function: they allow children to feel powerful and in control, creating safety and order out of danger and chaos.

Superhero and happy kitty stories very much mirror the kinds of pretend play that preschoolers frequently enjoy. Many boys enjoy pretending to be superheroes like Spider-Man, Batman, and Power Rangers, while many girls enjoy pretending to be kittens, puppies, ponies, and princesses. These differing interests are naturally reflected in their respective stories. (The role of gender in children's stories is discussed in more detail in chapter 12.)

The Power Rangers were red, blue, pink, green, and another blue. The Power Rangers fight the bad guys. They kicked and they falled down and bumped their heads. They went into their cave. The Power Rangers went in too. The Power Rangers popped out the bad guys.

Chris, age 4

The Princess and the Kitten

A kitten is lost. The princess finds the kitten. And the princess and the kitten went to play together. They play together in a really beautiful castle. The

Dictated stories about superheroes are often directly related to children's pretend play.

kitten and the princess were very happy in the castle. And the kitten eats
kitten food and the princess eats vanilla ice cream.
Sheri, age 4

Sometimes these two kinds of stories merge into one, such as when a princess
acts like a superhero. Here's an example.

The Princess
Once there was a princess. And then she got killed by a big vampire. Then
a different princess saved the other princess. She killed the vampire. The
princess who got killed said, "Let's play."
Kathy, age 4

If we substitute Spider-Man for princess in this story, we can't tell the difference between this story and a typical superhero story.

Although happy kitty stories usually are not as violent as superhero stories,
both provide the same satisfying resolution of conflict and danger.

There was a little and big sister. The little sister was Lisa. The big sister was
Megan. They played ghost monster in their house. One of the ghosts turned
into a real ghost dolly. The Care Bears were right in the rooms. They turned
into vampires. The vampires and the ghosts were just costumes. They were
playing ghost vampires.

Sarah, age 4

The author of this story creates danger and peril by turning the dolly into a
ghost and the Care Bears into vampires. But she quickly takes control, restoring
safety and order by explaining that it was all just a game. Superhero stories usually are more direct in their descriptions of the power of good over evil, though,
which is why they (and superhero play) are so satisfying to young children: they
clearly demonstrate their power over fearful situations.

Power Ranger he jump. Yellow. Red. And pink. A monster want to fight.
The Power Ranger hit the monster in the head. Pink say, "Stupid" to the
monster. Yellow say, "Shut up." The monster ran away.

Brian, age 4

Happy kitty stories may appear to be more gentle and peaceful than superhero
stories, but the body count can be just as high. Fortunately, those who die usually
come back to life again. Just as in children's pretend play, the dead will rise again,
refreshed, as if from a nap. Although children from ages three to five may not fully
understand the meaning of death, they are afraid of it and take it very seriously.
Bringing their characters back to life helps them grapple with this great unknown.

The princess rided on a unicorn to the castle. Then she saw a person who
had a pet pony. The unicorn and the pony loved each other and then they
died. The princess and the person were sad. Then the pony and the unicorn
came back. The princess married the prince.

Kathy, age 4

The Barbie died and the prince got her up. And then the mean old witch
fought Princess Barbie. Then some snow came down in the castle. Princess
Barbie and the prince got married.

Amy, age 3

Sometimes the storyteller takes a shortcut. Not bothering to create danger, death, or conflict, the author of this story goes straight to the domestic bliss typical of happy kitty stories.

> Once upon a time there was a princess and she lived in a castle. She looked out the window and she saw some birds. She said hello. Someone heard her. It was an elephant!
> *Karin, age 4*

Although fear and conflict are not directly expressed in this story, the telling of it allows the child to be in control, to create a happy situation and outcome.

Violence in Superhero Stories

Sometimes teachers and child care providers are uncomfortable with superhero stories because they think the stories are too violent. My experience has been that telling superhero stories—which, after all, describe pretend violence—actually helps children become more focused and productive rather than more violent. The violence in these stories is rather like the old Batman comic books, full of "pows" and "bangs" but with very little actual bloodshed. (Stories that include descriptions of actual gore and injuries are unusual; they are addressed in chapter 13.) The majority of the superhero stories that children dictate should not be cause for concern.

On the other hand, acting out superhero stories that contain violence can present special challenges. As described in chapter 6, if we decide to allow children to act out stories that contain fighting or violence, we must set clear limits on how the stories can be performed. Children as young as three usually are able to understand that pretend fighting means no touching. Any child who isn't able to follow this rule shouldn't be allowed to participate. But as noted previously, children are usually so strongly motivated by their desire to participate in acting out superhero stories that they're able to follow the rules and stay safe.

Repetition of Superhero Stories

Because some superheroes hold such special power for young children, it isn't surprising that a child may tell the same story over and over again, especially if he's repeating something he's seen in a movie or on television. If this is the case

One day, Frodo and Sam had to pack up their stuff. "So, Mr. Frodo, let's go on a fight," said Sam.

Children often include violence in superhero stories, but their descriptions are usually very basic and include little detail.

with a child in your charge, you may want to step in and gently encourage him to try creating his own superhero. I believe that if children are going to fully feel the personal satisfaction and benefits of telling a story about a powerful figure, they need to find ways to make that story their own so that it truly expresses their own feelings and ideas. Because it's easy to feel overwhelmed by the influence of mass media on children, I always feel encouraged when children create stories with powerful characters and images that aren't from television or movies. In the following story, a young boy clearly expresses his own satisfying feelings of power and accomplishment without using a television character.

> Firehouse. Fire go out. Me firefighter.
> *Aiden, age 3*

Here's another example, this one from an older boy who has created a story with his own unique and powerful characters.

Two ships were ruling the world. One was a submarine and one floated on top of the water. Then when two people were riding on a truck they saw two scuba divers. A construction boat and scuba divers fixed the bridge. There was this cute little frog so scuba divers scuba-ed down to rain forest. The end.

Matt, age 4

One of the best ways to encourage children to create unique and expressive stories with powerful characters is to expose them to a wide variety of high-quality books and stories. We must provide rich and interesting alternatives to the narrow and stereotypical cast of characters portrayed on television and in movies. Children can be just as entertained by characters who are role models for being powerful and positive. (In Appendix C, you'll find a list of children's books that can help children make the transition from television/movie superheroes to heroes in books.)

Exposing children to a wide variety of books encourages them to think about stories in different ways.

Heroes and Underdogs

Early childhood professionals may have differing views about superheroes, but we can all agree that children need positive role models. By definition, heroes should be admired for their achievements and noble qualities. Besides reading books about heroes to children, we can use the children's own stories to help emphasize positive behaviors. As you listen to children dictate their stories, look for examples of heroic acts and great kindnesses, as in the first story below, or unlikely triumphs of an underdog over a bully, as in the second.

> There was a wizard who fixed legs so they were not broken. The wizard had a special computer that told him whenever someone broke their leg or arm and a little light beeped. The wizard helped lots of kids. There weren't really doctors at that point. It was a long time ago when a particular war happened.
> *Neal, age 5*

> A dog comes. The kitty was angry. The kitty bited the dog. It wasn't a puppy, it was a big, huge dog. The dog went home.
> *Sara, age 4*

When children tell stories about heroism, bravery, or kindness, the way we react to their stories demonstrates to them how much we value those behaviors. Don't be afraid to praise positive behaviors described in a child's story. If a child has written a story about a positive role model, like the wizard who fixed legs, you might read the story aloud to the children and highlight the positive behaviors. You could then display the story prominently on a bulletin board and refer to it again when children experience real-life conflicts. You might say, "Remember Neal's story about the wizard who helped people? Maybe you could be like the wizard and help Daniel get his shoes on?" This kind of positive reinforcement helps to create and nurture a classroom or child care environment in which children treat each other with respect and consideration.

TEACHING TIPS

- Allow, even encourage, children to tell stories about monsters. Don't be concerned if such stories aren't resolved with happy endings.

- Don't automatically discourage stories about superheroes, even if they contain some violence. Such stories allow children to feel powerful and in control of their fears.

- Praise children's stories that describe positive social behavior. Use these stories to teach children how to get along with each other.

Gender and Culture in Stories

12

Gender and culture are important elements in the development of a sense of identity. This chapter examines the ways in which gender and culture influence children's storytelling and offers suggestions for using the storytelling process to support children's sense of identity.

Gender and Stories

Most early childhood teachers and providers agree that, in general, there are significant differences between the stories girls tell and the stories boys tell. Although not likely to be especially noticeable when children first begin telling stories as two- and three-year-olds, the differences are usually very significant by the time they're four or five. As we discussed in the previous chapter, boys tend to tell action stories about superheroes and other popular media characters. Girls may also be influenced by popular media, but their stories often center on animals, princesses, and families.

> Sleeping Beauty rides the Barbie bike. She goes to the wedding. She sees her father.
> *Sarah, age 3*

> Bad guys climbed over mountains. The Power Rangers kicked. The bad
> guys died.
> *Alex, age 3*

Developmentally, four- and five-year-olds are working hard to understand gender roles. Although children as young as two years old are able to identify their own gender, children usually do not master gender stability—the concept that one's gender will stay the same over time—until they're around age four. Furthermore, gender constancy—the idea that one's own gender remains the same regardless of changes to outside appearance—does not emerge until age five or six. A natural and unavoidable part of this learning process is belief in stereotypical gender roles. Even with the advances in gender equality over the last several decades, four- and five-year-olds often still believe in gender stereotypes—for example, that all girls play house or that all boys like to get dirty—even when directly confronted by contradictory evidence. We can liken it to the toddler who, when first learning about living creatures in the world, labels every animal dog, be it a cat, a squirrel, a horse, or a goat. As children learn, their thinking expands and becomes more flexible, allowing them to understand that there are differences among girls and boys, just as there are differences among animals and other forms of life.

While there are exceptions, these stereotypes are especially strong around ages four and five. A boy can't ride a pink bike. A girl can't wear Spider-Man pajamas. Stereotypes influence not only children's interests and pretend play but also the stories they dictate. Vivian Gussin Paley addresses these issues at length in her book *Boys and Girls: Superheroes in the Doll Corner.* "Every year, the girls begin with stories of good little families, while the boys bring us a litany of superheroes and bad guys. This kind of storytelling is an adjunct of play" (1984, p. 3).

Since we, as early childhood professionals, understand that these stereotypes are a natural and normal part of childhood, we can do much to assist children in their learning so that they eventually abandon such generalizations. We can begin by looking for opportunities to challenge stereotypic thinking and encourage critical thinking.

One way to challenge gender stereotypes is to randomly assign roles when children act out their stories in a group. You might, for example, go around the circle clockwise and assign roles in that order. If the characters in the story are a

Young children explore gender roles during pretend play.

superhero, a nurse, a fireman, and a kitty, you would assign the first child the role of the superhero, the second the role of the nurse, and so on, regardless of a child's gender. This way, boys will have the opportunity to play roles typically assigned to girls and vice versa. Although some children will pass on some roles, most children are eager to play any role. Assigning children to roles regardless of their gender helps them to think critically about gender stereotypes and to expand their thinking. If this sort of dramatization is practiced regularly over any length of time, teachers and child care providers usually begin to see less and less evidence of stereotypical gender roles in children's stories and play.

> The sun was out. And all the trees started to grow. And then Katie came with a swimsuit on and she splashed into the water. Then Superman came. Then some water splashed. Then the water splashed all over Katie and Superman.
> *Katie, age 4*

Culture and Identity in Dictated Stories

Because families play such an important role in children's stories, it makes sense that children's dictated stories are influenced by their family's culture and traditions.

> Mama cook the dumplings. Hot dumplings. Everybody eat them. Papa,
> Nana, and cousin Michael.
> *Lily, age 3*

Culture is, of course, much more than food and holiday traditions. On a deeper level, it includes values and beliefs, patterns of communication, and child-rearing practices. Sometimes the evidence of a child's culture can be found in how the child tells a story rather than in its content.

Researchers like Shirley Brice Heath (in Engel 1999, p. 46) have studied the many differences between cultures when it comes to language and storytelling. In the American educational system, children are taught based on a Eurocentric perspective about the purpose, structure, and language of stories: the plotline of the story is linear; it has a beginning, a middle, and an end. A story has one or two main characters who encounter a conflict, and the story ends when the conflict has been resolved.

> Cinderella made a dress. She went to the ball in a carriage. Then when ugly
> stepsisters saw her, they tore her dress. She ran down the stairs and lost her
> glass slipper. Then the prince and Cinderella lived happily ever after.
> *Sonya, age 5*

In many non-European cultures, however, stories can be organized in a very different way. Stories might be about several main characters who have experiences related to the same theme. In cultures that value interdependence more than independence, a child's story might focus more on the needs and feelings of characters besides the narrator (Curenton 2006). This young child's story focuses on the actions and needs of other family members.

> I love Mama and I love Daddy and I love Grandpa. My Mama laugh. She
> sing a song sometimes. Daddy play the radio. Everyone has to be quiet
> because Grandpa sleeping.
> *Kiki, age 3*

When we keep in mind that children's stories are influenced by culture and that the Eurocentric way is not the only way to tell a story, we are better able to listen to children's dictated stories with an open, unbiased attitude.

Including English-Language Learners

Good teachers know how important it is that every child feel included in the learning community. Every child may not choose to dictate stories, but every child should feel welcome to do so, especially if that child is learning to speak English.

Nowhere is the topic of developing children's language skills more relevant or more urgent than in our work with children who are learning English as a second language. Approximately 10 percent of all children in public prekindergarten settings and more than 25 percent of children in Head Start settings speak a language other than English at home. And those numbers are steadily rising. By 2010, more than 30 percent of all school children will come from homes where English is not the primary language (NAEYC 2006). The National Association for the Education of Young Children recommends that early childhood providers make every effort to use children's home languages and to create learning environments that reflect children's languages and cultures.

In keeping with these NAEYC recommendations, it is important that children who are learning English have opportunities to tell stories in both their home language and in English.

> Mi padre me llevo al parquet.
> *Julissa, age 4*

> I see TV at home. Me, brother, Mom, and Dad watch TV at home. Me, brother, Mom, and Dad don't want to watch TV anymore. Janie press the button and close the TV. Janie and brother went upstairs to go to sleep.
> *Janie, age 4 (dictating in English, her second language)*

Ideally, a child's first experience dictating stories will be in that child's home language. The stories children tell in their home language almost always will be more complex and detailed than stories they tell in a second language. Intuitively, it makes sense that words and ideas flow more smoothly when a child speaks in the language he's most familiar with.

At the Child Development Center of the Chinese American Service League, an agency that serves Chinese immigrants in Chicago, children have the opportunity to dictate stories in both Chinese and English. A child may dictate a story in Chinese one day and a story in English on another. Teachers at this center have found that a child's first story in English usually consists of only a word or two, perhaps just "Daddy," whereas the child's first story in Chinese may be much longer, perhaps "Daddy went to work. Daddy waved good-bye. I love my Daddy." The children act out both their Chinese stories and their English stories. The center's teachers believe the dramatization process is especially important because it helps children to visualize words and concepts that are new to them.

Children who are English-language learners benefit greatly from opportunities to dictate stories in their home language.

Not every preschool or child care program has staff capable of writing down children's stories in their home language. For that reason, many programs must recruit volunteers. (The use of volunteers for story dictation is discussed in chapter 4. The handouts in Appendix B can be used to help train volunteers.) Because story dictation is one of the best methods for children to practice using language, the extra effort required to recruit volunteers who speak a home language is well worth it. In any language, story dictation allows children to practice using new vocabulary words without the pressure of meeting specific teacher-directed expectations, and children gain the satisfying sense of accomplishment that comes from seeing their words appear on paper.

When transcribing stories dictated in a child's home language is impossible, you have several options. One is to have the child draw a picture instead of telling a story. The child may then be able to respond to a request, such as "Tell me about this picture. What is this?" as you point at the drawing. If so, you can label the drawing with a few English words.

Another option is to have the child act out a story with dolls or puppets while you write down your observations of the dramatization. For example, based on observing a child's play, you might write, "The baby was crying. The mommy rocked the baby. Then the baby went to sleep."

Beyond its effectiveness as a tool for language development, there is a second critical reason why children who are learning English benefit from the story dictation process. The reason is that children who enter an English-speaking classroom (as well as an English-speaking community and society) without being able to speak and understand English are at risk of not being heard. It's difficult enough for any child to make her voice heard over the clamor of children in a busy classroom or child care setting. It's even more difficult for an English language learner to experience the affirmation of someone truly listening to her. We must be sure we give the most vulnerable children in our care the gift of our full attention, becoming all ears for the few short minutes it takes to receive their stories.

Story Dictation in a Culturally Relevant and Antibias Curriculum

This is me.
Anton, age 4

Story dictation is an important tool for early childhood professionals seeking to make their curriculum more responsive and meaningful to the diverse population of children and families represented in their classrooms, programs, and communities. It can support our efforts to help children develop a strong and positive identity and feel comfortable interacting with all kinds of people.

Antibias work is an active approach to challenging prejudice, stereotyping, and bias, and those who practice a culturally relevant and antibias (sometimes called *CRAB)* approach value human diversity and the fair treatment of all people (Derman-Sparks 1989).

For those who are already practicing a CRAB approach, as well as for those who are just beginning to explore antibias curricula, story dictation can be a meaningful and fruitful practice. Dictated stories can be authentic expressions of a child's identity, interests, and ideas, and they can be shared among children in a way that promotes acceptance and learning.

Here are the first two goals of a CRAB curriculum:

1. To support each child's construction of a knowledgeable, confident self and group identity.
2. To foster the development of comfortable, empathic interactions with people from diverse backgrounds.

(Bisson Hohensee and Derman-Sparks 1992; reprinted with permission from Louise Derman-Sparks, with one edit to the first goal, personal communication, August 30, 2006)

Stories Support the Construction of Identity

Story dictation can be an especially rich and valuable way of supporting the development of a child's unique voice and sense of self, thus supporting the first antibias goal. When children dictate stories about their family, interests, and how they spend their time, they are telling the story of who they are.

> One day I was walking in the woods with my family. Then I went to the
> park with my papa. Then I went to my house to get some candy. Then
> my papa took me riding on a bike. Then my mommy put everything she
> needed in a backpack. She did everything to pack me up.
> *Timothy, age 4*

In this story, the child is exploring his identity by describing his relationship to his parents, his favorite foods, and the activities his family enjoys. This process of describing actually helps the child construct an identity for himself.

Story dictation also provides a safe place for children to explore different aspects of their self-concept, as they try on different roles and personas.

> I'm shooting the basket and it scored. Michael Jordan, Shaquille O'Neal,
> and Jonathan, we played and jumped.
> *Jonathan, age 4*

In this story, the child describes some of the qualities and skills he admires, particularly physical abilities. Through this story, he explores who he is, what he values, and also who he wishes to become. These are all important parts of self-identity, and exploring them can help the child think about how his values may be similar to or different from the values of others.

Stories Help Children Understand Each Other

Every time a child shares a story with others by speaking it out loud, by acting it out in front of a group, or by allowing the teacher to publish it and thus have it be read by others, that child is sharing an authentic part of herself with others. This sharing of stories supports the second antibias goal, which is to foster the development of comfortable, empathic interactions with people from diverse backgrounds.

> I love my family. And they always buy me food. And they have a dojo and when you have a birthday and you have people over to the dojo and you eat. We do karate with our cousins. And we do exercise. And you say words after you do karate. And we have chocolate and we have tea. And we do some dressing clothes cuz we going somewhere. We go to church to see people a little while and then we leave. And we bake potatoes and we bake ice cream.
>
> *Jeanie, age 4*

This story is probably a pretty accurate description of Jeanie's family activities. For children who haven't had the same experiences Jeanie has had, such as visiting a dojo (a school where karate is taught), or learning karate, or going to church, hearing Jeanie's story opens a window into a new world. Sharing stories about family life allows children to look at both the similarities among and the differences between people.

Even among children from the same cultural group, the sharing of stories can help develop understanding and empathy. Suppose a teacher reads aloud the following story.

> Me and Papa went fishing. I saw worms.
>
> *Daniel, age 3*

Regardless of what background they come from, the children who hear this story will experience it as a window into another child's life, learning about a tradition that is important in that child's family. Exposure to the ideas and experiences of other children through the sharing of stories helps children understand each other better and become more empathetic in their interactions with others.

TEACHING TIPS

- When acting out stories, children should be assigned roles at random, regardless of gender. Seeing boys play female roles and girls play male roles helps challenge children's thinking about gender stereotypes.

- Create opportunities for children who are learning English to dictate stories in their home language. If necessary, recruit volunteers to take dictation or translate the stories.

- Use children's dictated stories to spark a discussion about families. Read aloud several different dictated stories about families and ask children, "How are our families the same?" and "How are our families different?"

- As one way to help children develop an understanding of other children's experiences, take a child's story that includes a number of different roles and have a group of children act it out several times, each time with those children in different roles. This gives children the opportunity to see a story from several different perspectives.

13

When Children's Stories Cause Concern

Sometimes a child will tell a story that makes us feel uncomfortable. This is usually because the child has used language or created images that we feel are unsuitable for young children or that indicate potentially serious underlying issues. These images often involve violence or sex. In some cases, a story may lead us to suspect problems at home, such as abuse. This chapter suggests guidelines for determining what topics and images are cause for concern and offers strategies for responding to troublesome stories.

"I think I'll drink my wine," said Emma.

Some stories contain images that we may find unsuitable for young children.

Violence and Sex in Children's Stories

As described in chapter 11, children's stories about superheroes are likely to include violence. Batman punches an alien, the Power Rangers kick the evil scientists, and Rescue Heroes crush the robbers with a pile of rocks. Often the violence is comic book–style violence, full of action and slapstick, but with little actual bloodshed. This kind of violence usually doesn't concern us.

What can cause concern is violence in a child's story that includes realistic descriptions of bloodshed, injuries, and wounds. I would be especially concerned if the story is written in the first person and the violence takes place in the child's home or involves the child's family. A clear example would be a child's story that describes a gun or guns in a realistic context, such as the child's home.

> The bad guy, he stole my stuff. He stole my gun and my money and my phone. I'm not going to let nobody take my stuff. He stole my glasses. And he stole my rap clothes. My rap shirt is green and red. I tried to go over to his house and take my gun and money and my rap shirt and my glasses and my phone. He wasn't there. So I opened the door with my key and there was a witch in there. I went to sleep and when he came in I poo-pooed in my pants. He got a big stick and he whipped me on the head. I took my gun and my sword and shoot and cut him.
>
> *Tim, age 4*

Even if we know that this little boy is making some of this up, we should wonder if other elements of his story are based on true experiences. Might this child have been severely punished for soiling his pants? Has he seen a real gun in his home? There's no way to know for sure just from reading this story. We'd need to inquire further to find out whether there's cause for concern.

We also need to pay special attention if there is sexual language or imagery in a story. By this I do not mean children's developmentally appropriate bathroom humor or potty talk. It's not unusual for children to be interested in peeing and pooping and to have a natural curiosity about the body parts that create pee and poop. But we should be concerned if a child tells a story about his or her genitals being touched by someone or about touching someone else's genitals. Similarly, whereas general talk about babies and having babies is appropriate for young children, a child's story describing explicit sexual behavior is not.

Here's an example of a story by a little boy that raises questions about the child's knowledge of and experience with sex.

> I have three and five girlfriends. I tried to touching or something. I tried to play with my girls. When I go home I tried to sleep with my girls. When we wake up we are going to play with the Play Station. I need to help my girls play games so I can't kill the monster so I can be finish and let my girls play.
>
> *Evan, age 4*

This story, along with other supporting evidence, caused the child's teachers to be concerned that he had been exposed to pornography.

Talking with Young Children

What is a teacher or child care provider to do upon hearing a story like this? First of all, you must offer an immediate response when a child finishes telling such a story. You want to communicate to the child that you are listening and that you accept what he has to say. A comment like "I'm very interested in the story you just told me" shows the child that you've heard his story and that you value it. What comes next depends on the situation. If you have enough time and privacy for a conversation about the story, it might be wise to ask the child a few open-ended questions. It usually isn't helpful to ask a point-blank question such as, "Is any of this true?" because three- to five-year-olds are too young to distinguish between fact and fiction in their stories. If a child feels the emotions of a story strongly, then it's all true to him. A more effective approach might be to put your pencil down, look at the child, and say, "I'd like to know more about this story. Tell me about the witch." Or "Tell me about the gun." Perhaps the child's response will provide some clues about the origins of the story. Perhaps not. Do not press the child to talk more if he's reluctant to do so. Let the child know that you're available to talk about the story at any time. Of course, if you suspect the child may be in danger, you must act immediately.

Seek Support

After you have talked with the child, seek out a colleague, supervisor, mentor, or another person with whom you can confidentially discuss your concerns. A child's story that contains violent or disturbing images raises many questions. Should you discuss the story with the child's family, and if so, how? Does the story indicate that something is wrong and needs to be addressed? Might this child have been exposed to or experienced things that are not appropriate for him? Is this child in some kind of danger? These are not questions to be pondered alone. Consulting a social worker or mental health expert often provides helpful support.

What If You Suspect Abuse?

Early childhood professionals have the legal and ethical responsibility to report suspected abuse and neglect to child welfare authorities. If, as part of story dictation, a child makes a direct statement such as "My mommy whipped me with a big stick," the teacher or child care provider must report it. In my experience, however, children are not likely to make a direct statement regarding abuse or neglect while dictating a story.

What is more likely is that a child tells a story that makes her teacher or child care provider feel uneasy, and that story, combined with other significant input, such as observations of the child's behavior and play and information gleaned from informal conversations between child and teacher, eventually leads to some kind of action, such as a report of suspected abuse or a referral for mental health services. Sometimes the story is the tipping point, the final straw that convinces a teacher or provider to take action. And sometimes a child's story is the reason a teacher starts taking notes and watching for other signs of abuse or neglect.

In the case of Evan, the author of the story about the "three and five girl-friends," teachers already had concerns, based on his play and conversations, before he dictated his story. And because he and his family were already receiving intervention services at the time the story was dictated, it did not lead to any specific action. The story did, however, reinforce the teachers' concerns and provide supporting evidence of Evan's exposure to inappropriate material.

Unless it contains direct statements about abuse or neglect, a single dictated story is probably not enough reason to report abuse or initiate some other kind of significant intervention. A disturbing story told by a troubled child usually is not surprising to a teacher who already knows the child. Such a story usually is just one small window into a larger problem. In these situations, it is always important to consult with other classroom teachers or child care providers, as well as with social workers or mental health professionals.

Another Possibility to Consider

An additional possibility must be considered when a child's story seems disturbing. Because preschool children are always experimenting with words and language, they often use words and phrases they don't fully understand. For example, a child in the block corner who says she's building a "contraction" really means "contraption." It is possible that a dictated story perceived by a teacher as disturbing could instead be a benign and random combination of words, phrases, and ideas that a child has cobbled together from sources as varied as television shows, advertisements, and overheard conversations. Consider this example of a story that might cause a teacher or child care provider to be concerned.

> Once upon a time there was a girl who lived with a monster. The monster was so nasty to her. And he didn't do anything to her, just complain to her. And he hit her. And he be bad to her. And he put a staple in her. And he put another staple in. And he made a dark sky. And it poured and poured. That's the end.
>
> *Robin, age 3*

Not knowing the child, one could read this story and suspect the child was being physically abused and that the monster might represent a possible abuser. However, because I know this child and her family well and I also know that she is an experienced storyteller with a vivid imagination, I am convinced that this is just a simple monster story.

Telling a disturbing story doesn't necessarily mean that a child is disturbed. In fact, without some understanding of the context in which a story is told, it's almost impossible to know the true meaning of a child's story.

Talking with Parents

Although you may feel reluctant about sharing an especially violent or disturbing story, with very few exceptions, stories should be shared with parents. In fact, as discussed previously, there is great value in sharing the stories children dictate with parents and families as part of a regular routine. When you share stories with parents on a regular basis, it is then easier to initiate a discussion about a story that concerns you. What you're likely to find is that most parents agree with the parent who once said to me, "I want to know everything important that goes on at school. My child's stories are a big part of that."

When approaching a parent to discuss a story that has caused you concern, make sure the conversation takes place in a private area, away from the children and other parents. Depending on the seriousness of your concerns, you may want to ask your supervisor or another staff member to join you. You might begin by presenting the story for the parent to read first, perhaps by saying, "Meagan dictated a story today that I thought you'd want to see." After the parent reads the story, you can state your concern about it and ask, in an open-ended way, for a response: "I was surprised that Meagan's story included so many violent details. What are your thoughts about it?" How you proceed, of course, depends on many different factors. Hopefully, you and the parent can work together to determine if any further action may be necessary.

There are times when you should not show stories to parents. If you have reason to believe that a child will be punished for something revealed in a story, such as sensitive information about family members, or provocative language being spoken, or something illegal taking place in the home, you should not show the story. If for any reason you're afraid a child will be punished for dictating a specific story, consult with a supervisor or mental health professional to come up with a plan for how to communicate with the family about the content of their child's story.

Would you show the following story to a parent?

> This is the day when I sleep at night. And a rat comes running down the
> slide and a boy came and tried to kill it. And a rainbow came shining down
> and the butterflies came flying and the flowers come up and I love the
> whole world except my family.
> *Marina, age 4*

What parent would enjoy reading "I love the whole world except my family"? In this case, I knew this child did indeed love her family very much. I wasn't sure why she dictated those words in her story, but I knew that it would cause her mother pain to read them. In general, I would consider not showing such a story to a parent only if I were sure it was an odd fluke, not part of a larger pattern. If a child frequently told stories like this one, I would feel the need, after gaining support from my supervisor and colleagues, to discuss the stories with the parent.

The Healing Power of Story Dictation

Unless the story opens up issues we don't feel qualified to address, we shouldn't be afraid to provide additional opportunities for storytelling to a child who's told a disturbing story. Story dictation can be a very helpful process for a troubled child. The child may gain comfort and encouragement from the experience of being heard and understood. Also, the stories may be helpful to family members and mental health professionals who are trying to better understand the child and her struggles.

Although the settings we work in may not be labeled *therapeutic,* ordinary preschool classrooms and family child care settings are places in which healing and growth take place every day. A trusting relationship between caregiver and child is the essential ingredient. Each time we give a child our full attention and invite that child to tell us his story, we provide a safe place for healing and growth. Story dictation, though not a replacement for mental health services, can be a valuable supplement for children who are already receiving outside support.

The Importance of Reflection

Children benefit greatly when teachers are willing to take the time to reflect on the content and meaning of their stories and seek a deeper understanding of them through their stories. Jane Katch beautifully illustrates the power of a teacher's reflections in her book *Under Deadman's Skin: Discovering the Meaning of Children's Violent Play,* which describes teacher Katch's struggle to understand the violence in young children's play and language. Through her careful and sensitive reflections, Katch develops the hypothesis that the most powerful tool available to teachers in understanding children is empathy (Ketch 2001). The process of listening to children's dictated stories is an important opportunity to nurture our own abilities to reflect, understand, and empathize with the children in our care.

TEACHING TIPS

- Share children's stories with parents on a regular basis. Doing so makes it much easier to discuss your concern about a particular story with parents if the need arises.

- If a child's story causes you concern, discuss it confidentially with a supervisor, a colleague, or a mental health expert.

- When a child's story makes you feel uncomfortable, consider the possibility that it may be the result of the child randomly combining words, phrases, and images. Or perhaps the child unintentionally viewed a television show, movie, or advertisement intended for adults. Even children of cautious and vigilant parents sometimes are exposed to images that have sexual or violent content.

Conclusion:
Readers and Writers of the Future

I often feel a quiet sense of urgency about capturing young children's stories on paper. The urgency is a result of understanding that as children grow older, they lose much of their ability and desire to spontaneously and creatively invent their own stories. As young children begin learning the formal conventions of writing in elementary school, they often become self-conscious about their words and ideas and repress much of the spontaneity and creativity that was theirs when they were younger. The American poet Sharon Olds says that every child is born a poet, but "the gift of writing, the ability to write poetry is something that has to be actively taken away from you. Which our culture's happy to do, as most cultures are" (in Kusnetz 2006).

As an example, consider the story of child poet Hilda Conkling. Born in 1910, Hilda was the daughter of the poet Grace Hazard Conkling. Around age 4, Hilda began dictating poems to her mother. The little girl's poetry became widely known for its fresh and creative imagery, and in 1920 a book of Hilda's poetry, *Poems by a Little Girl*, was published. When Hilda became a teenager, her mother refused to continue taking dictation, insisting that Hilda write down her own poems. Interestingly, Hilda refused and abruptly stopped composing poems. Perhaps there was something about the dictation process that allowed Hilda to be free and inventive with language, something she was unable or unwilling to do once she had to do her own writing.

The time period that begins the moment a child starts speaking in full sentences and ends the moment that child begins learning the formal conventions of writing is a unique window of opportunity for creative storytelling before children become self-conscious. Although many school-age children enjoy using their newly acquired writing skills to write their own stories, it's important that we continue to provide opportunities for them to dictate stories and tap into their uninhibited imaginations.

Many children continue to enjoy making up their own stories after they've learned to write independently.

Esme Raji Codell, author of many children's books, including *Diary of a Fairy Godmother, Sing a Song of Tuna Fish, Sahara Special,* and *Vive La Paris,* explains a similar experience from when she was very young.

> *When I was six, I still hadn't learned to read, mostly by force of will. I didn't want to learn, because I was afraid that if I did, people would stop reading to me! My clever teacher asked me what I would like to write a book about. And if I said "a chicken" or "a flower" or what-all, she cut out the shape as best she could from construction paper and blank writing paper and stapled it together, like a "real" paperback. Then I would dictate my story to her, and she would print very clearly on the inside sheets, leaving me room to illustrate. But I had to know what the words said before I knew what to draw, and I certainly wanted to share my story when I was all done. In this way, I learned to read using books I had written. The experience of story dictation made a powerful connection between books and the ability to communicate that has never left me.* (Codell, pers. comm.)

As Codell's story makes clear, it's important that we allow children to continue to dictate stories, even after they've developed the ability to read and write. Young children find value in the story dictation process beyond the simple writing of words. For them, story dictation is about stretching their imaginations, having an attentive listener who records their words, and building a warm and trusting relationship with their caregiver.

Codell's story also suggests that a future poet or author may be sitting at your writing table today, waiting to dictate a story to you. Story dictation benefits all children, but for some it reveals gifts that allow them to blossom. This was the first story dictated by a four-year-old child.

> One time I was coming back from a water park to my RV and when I was walking over a bridge I fell. And then my daddy was so scared he dropped everything that was in his hand and ran over to me.
> *Sabine, age 4*

This story of a family outing isn't unusual, but the freedom and ease in the child's use of language is extraordinary for a young child with no experience in dictating stories. By including a few key details ("he dropped everything that was in his hand"), she captures the drama of a single moment. Her sentences are quite complex, the meaning beautifully clear. At age four, this child is able to accomplish what college-level writing instructors are always asking of their students: show, don't tell. The story sprang from this child's mouth, fully formed and complete. Regular opportunities to dictate will no doubt nurture and document the development of her talents.

Pay Attention

The story dictation process invites children to pay attention to their world in a deeper way and to pay attention to each other when stories are read aloud. It also invites us teachers and child care providers to pay attention to children with respect and interest.

Because people are by nature storytellers, there's something about the process of taking an idea or experience and calling it a story that makes all of us take notice. When I was a preschool teacher and it was time to take the children outside to the playground, our ritual was to gather at the door with our jackets on and take a moment to review our playground safety rules. Invariably, the children were so eager to go outside that they had trouble listening to anything I had to say about rules. On a day when the children were especially restless, I announced, "Once upon a time!" Suddenly, a hush fell over the room, and every pair of eyes was on me. I went on, "Once upon a time there was a class called the Red Room, and every day they went outside to the playground. The children in the Red Room knew they had to stay safe, so this is what they did: they held hands with a partner while they were walking. When they got to the playground, they went down the slide and never up the slide. They dug holes in the sand and did not throw the sand. And they lived happily ever after. The end." When I finished my story, every child was smiling at me and ready to go outside. By turning the rules into a story, I'd convinced the children to pay attention to what I had to say.

Stories invite us to pay attention in many different ways. The child storyteller pays attention to words and ideas when he creates the story. The teacher pays attention to the child as the story is dictated. And all who enjoy the sharing of the story, from the children sitting on the rug to the family reading the bulletin board, are paying attention to something very important—the building of a richer relationship among all concerned. It is this giving of attention at so many different levels that makes story dictation such a rich and magical process.

Appendix A: Instructions for Volunteers

On the following pages, you'll find a reproducible letter that you can give to
volunteer scribes to introduce them to story dictation. An English version of the
letter appears on page 152 and a Spanish version appears on page 153.

Dear Volunteer,

Thank you for volunteering to help with story dictation in our classroom!

Your role will be to serve as a "scribe" at our writing table during free play. You will write down the words the children say as they take turns telling stories. This activity is called "story dictation." In story dictation, a child tells a story (or simply describes an event or a person) and an adult writes down the child's words.

Start with a fresh sheet of paper for each story. Write the child's name and the date at the top of the page. Some children will want to try to write their own names, which is fine.

Tell the child, "I'm ready to write your story. How does it begin?" Write down the words exactly as the child says them. Don't worry about mistakes in grammar or sentences that don't make sense. The most important thing is that the child has the experience of seeing his or her words in print.

The children will probably talk faster than you can write. If the storyteller is speaking too fast, just say, "Slow down, please. I need more time to write down all your words." Read back what you have written so far, so the child knows how much you've written. It's okay to ask children to repeat what they said.

Some children's stories may be as short as one or two sentences. Other children will want to tell very long stories. It's a good idea to limit each story to one page.

Feel free to ask the teachers for help or to ask them questions during your time in the classroom.

Thank you for helping us with this important activity. Story dictation helps children learn about words and writing. It also encourages children's language and social development. We're glad you could be a part of it.

Sincerely,

Querido Voluntario,

¡Gracias por ofrecer su voluntariado para ayudar con el "Dictado de Cuentos" en nuestra clase!

Su trabajo será el de servir como un "escritor" en nuestra mesa de escritura durante el juego libre. Usted escribirá las palabras de los niños cuando ellos tomen turnos contando cuentos. Esto se llama "Dictado de Cuentos". En el Dictado de Cuentos un niño cuenta un cuento (o simplemente describe de un evento o a una persona) y un adulto escribe las palabras de los niños.

Comience con una hoja de papel para cada cuento. Escriba el nombre del niño y la fecha de hoy en la parte de superior de la página. Algunos niños querrán tratar de escribir sus propios nombres lo cual está bien que lo hagan.

Dígale al niño, "Ya estoy listo para escribir tu cuento. ¿Cómo empieza el cuento? Escriba las palabras exactamente como el niño las dice. No se preocupe acerca de los errores gramaticales o de las oraciones que no tengan sentido. Lo más importante es que el niño tenga la experiencia de ver sus propias palabras escritas.

Los niños probablemente hablarán más rápido de lo que usted escribe. Si el niño está hablando muy rápido, sólo dígale, "Más despacio, por favor. Necesito más tiempo para escribir todas tus palabras". Regrese y lea lo que ha escrito hasta ahora así que el niño sabrá en que parte del dictado usted va. Está bien pedirles a los niños que repitan lo que dijeron.

Algunos cuentos de los niños pueden ser de una o dos oraciones. A otros niños les gustará decir cuentos largos. Es una muy buena idea limitar cada cuento a una página.

Cuando usted esté en el salón de clase, siéntase libre de pedir ayuda o pedir a los maestros (as) que respondan a las preguntas que usted pueda tener.

Gracias por ayudarnos con esta actividad tan importante. El Dictado de Cuentos ayuda a los niños a aprender acerca de las palabras y la escritura. Esto también anima el desarrollo social y del lenguaje de los niños. Nosotros estamos encantados de que usted pueda ser parte de esto.

Atentamente,

Appendix B: Story Dictation Information for Parents and Families

On the following pages, you'll find a reproducible letter you can give to parents and families that describes how they can do story dictation at home. An English version of the letter appears on page 155 and a Spanish version appears on page 156.

Dear Families,

We would like to tell you about one of our classroom activities that helps to build children's language and literacy skills. It is called "story dictation." In story dictation, a child tells a story (or simply describes an event or a person), and an adult writes down what the child says. This activity helps children learn about words and writing. It also gives children an opportunity to be creative and use their imagination.

We will be sharing the children's stories with you on a regular basis. Younger children and children new to story dictation will probably tell stories that are very short, just a sentence or two. But as children gain more practice telling stories and develop more language skills, they eventually tell longer and more complicated stories. Our philosophy is that children should have the freedom to tell stories any way they choose. Some stories may be about ordinary daily events. Others may be about people and activities that the children imagine. Children usually enjoy sharing these stories with each other and with their families.

You may want to try story dictation at home. Invite your child to tell you a story. The story might be based on a happy memory. ("Tell me about the time Grandma took you to the zoo.") Or you could invite your child to re-tell, in his or her own words, a story from a favorite book or movie.

Write down the words exactly as your child says them. Don't worry about mistakes in grammar or sentences that don't make sense. The most important thing is that your child has the experience of seeing his or her words in print.

We invite you to bring to school any stories your child dictates at home. These stories are often really fun to read to the class.

If you have questions about story dictation, please don't hesitate to talk with us. You're also welcome to visit the classroom to observe or help with story dictation.

Sincerely,

Queridas Familias,

Nos gustaría decirles acerca de una de nuestras actividades en el salón de clase que ayuda a construir el lenguaje de los niños y las habilidades de lecto-escritura. Esta actividad se llama "Dictado de Cuentos". En este dictado un niño cuenta un cuento o historia (o simplemente describe un evento o a una persona) y un adulto escribe acerca de lo que dijo el niño. Esta es una actividad que ayuda a los niños a aprender acerca de las palabras y la escritura. Esto también da oportunidades a los niños para ser creativos y usar su imaginación.

Nosotros estaremos compartiendo los cuentos de los niños con usted regularmente. Los niños pequeños y los que apenas están conociendo el dictado probablemente nos dirán historias muy cortas de sólo una o dos oraciones. Pero cuando el niño empiece a tener más práctica dictando cuentos y desarrollando más habilidades de lenguaje, eventualmente contará cuentos un poquito más complicados y más largos. Nuestra filosofía es que los niños deben tener libertad para contar cuentos o historias en la manera que ellos quieran. Algunos cuentos serán acerca de sus experiencias diarias y otros pueden ser de personas y cosas que están en la imaginación de los niños. Los niños usualmente disfrutan al compartir estos cuentos con otros niños y con sus familias.

Usted quizás quiera intentar hacer un dictado de cuentos en su casa. Invite a su niño a que le cuente un cuento. A lo mejor el cuento puede ser basado en un recuerdo o experiencia feliz; por ejemplo usted puede decirle al niño "Cuéntame del día que tu abuelita te llevó al zoológico". O usted puede invitar al niño a que le recuente, con sus propias palabras, un cuento de su libro favorito o de una película.

Escriba las palabras como el niño exactamente las dice. No se preocupes acerca de los errores gramaticales u oraciones que no tengan sentido. Lo más importante es que el niño tenga la experiencia de ver sus propias palabras escritas.

Usted puede traer a la escuela cualquier cuento que su niño le haya dictado en casa. Estas historias son a menudo realmente divertidas para leerlas en el salón de clase.

Si usted tiene preguntas acerca del Dictado de Cuentos por favor no dude en hablar con nosotros.

Su visita al salón de clase es siempre bienvenida, ya bien sea para observar o para ayudar en el dictado de cuentos.

Atentamente,

Appendix C: Recommended Reading

Recommended Stories for Acting Out

Bruss, Deborah. 2001. *Book! Book! Book!* New York: Arthur A. Levine Books.

Burningham, John. 1970. *Mr. Gumpy's Outing.* New York: Holt, Reinhart and Winston.

Eastman, P. D. 1960. *Are You My Mother?* New York: Beginner Books.

Fleming, Denise. 1998. *Mama Cat Has Three Kittens.* New York: Henry Holt.

Forest, Heather. 1998. *Stone Soup.* Little Rock, Ark.: August House.

Galdone, Paul. 1970. *The Three Little Pigs.* New York: Seabury Press.

————. 1981. *The Three Billy Goats Gruff.* New York: Clarion Press.

Hutchins, Pat. 1968. *Rosie's Walk.* New York: Simon & Schuster.

Krauss, Ruth. 1945. *The Carrot Seed.* New York: Harper & Row.

Murphy, Mary. 2002. *How Kind!* Cambridge, Mass.: Candlewick Press.

Shannon, David. 2002. *Duck on a Bike.* New York: Blue Sky Press.

Slobodkina, Esphyr. 1968. *Caps for Sale: A Tale of a Peddler, Some Monkeys and Their Monkey Business.* Reading, Mass.: Young Scott Books.

Recommended Read-Aloud Picture Books

These picture books can help inspire young children to create their own imaginative stories.

Carle, Eric. 1987. *The Very Hungry Caterpillar.* New York: Philomel Books.

Falwell, Cathryn. 1993. *Feast for 10.* New York: Clarion Books.

Feiffer, Jules. 1999. *Bark, George.* New York: HarperCollins.

Fleming, Candace. 2002. *Muncha! Muncha! Muncha!* New York: Atheneum.

Fox, Mem. 1987. *Hattie and the Fox.* New York: Bradbury Press.

Gag, Wanda. 1928. *Millions of Cats.* New York: Coward-McCann.

Greenfield, Eloise. 1977. *Honey, I Love, and Other Love Poems.* New York: Crowell.

Henkes, Kevin. 2004. *Kitten's First Full Moon.* New York: Greenwillow Books.

Hoberman, Mary Ann. 1997. *The Seven Silly Eaters.* San Diego: Harcourt Brace.

Hogrogian, Nonny. 1971. *One Fine Day.* New York: Macmillan.

Keats, Ezra Jack. 1962. *The Snowy Day.* New York: Viking Press.

Kimmel, Eric A. 1988. *Anansi and the Moss-Covered Rock.* New York: Holiday House.

Kraus, Robert. 1970. *Whose Mouse Are You?* New York: Macmillan.

Lin, Grace. 2001. *Dim Sum for Everyone!* New York: Knopf.

Martin, Bill Jr. 1992. *Brown Bear, Brown Bear, What Do You See?* New York: Henry Holt.

Martin, Bill Jr., and John Archambault. 1989. *Chicka Chicka Boom Boom.* New York: Simon & Schuster.

McCloskey, Robert. 1941. *Make Way for Ducklings.* New York: Viking Press.

Osborne, Mary Pope. 2000. *Kate and the Beanstalk.* New York: Atheneum.

Rathmann, Peggy. 1994. *Good Night, Gorilla.* New York: Putnam.

Ringgold, Faith. 1991. *Tar Beach.* New York: Crown Publishers.

Rohman, Eric. 2002. *My Friend Rabbit.* Brookfield, Conn.: Roaring Brook Press.

Sendak, Maurice. 1963. *Where the Wild Things Are.* New York: Harper & Row.

———. 1970. *In the Night Kitchen.* New York: Harper & Row.

Shannon, David. 1998. *No, David!* New York: Blue Sky Press.

Shaw, Nancy. 1986. *Sheep in a Jeep.* Boston, Mass.: Houghton Mifflin.

Smith, Linda. 2002. *Mrs. Biddlebox.* New York: HarperCollins.

Steig, William. 1998. *Pete's a Pizza.* New York: HarperCollins.

Sturges, Philemon. 1999. *The Little Red Hen Makes a Pizza.* New York: Dutton.

Trivizas, Eugene, and Helen Oxenbury. 1993. *The Three Little Wolves and the Big Bad Pig.* New York: Maxwell Macmillan International.

Waddell, Martin. 1992. *Owl Babies.* Cambridge, Mass.: Candlewick Press.

Walter, Virginia. 1995. *Hi, Pizza Man!* New York: Orchard Books.

Willems, Mo. 2003. *Don't Let the Pigeon Drive the Bus.* New York: Hyperion.

Williams, Vera B. 1990. *"More More More," said the Baby.* New York: Greenwillow Books.

Wood, Audry. 1984. *The Napping House.* San Diego: Harcourt Brace Jovanovich.

Zimmerman, Andrea, and David Clemesha. 1999. *Trashy Town.* New York: HarperCollins.

Recommended Superhero Stories

Arnold, Tedd. 2006. *Super Fly Guy.* New York: Scholastic.

Auerbach, Annie. 2004. *Wildfire!* New York: Little Simon.

———. 2004. *Hero Copter.* New York: Little Simon.

Bogacki, Tomasz. 1998. *Cat and Mouse in the Night.* New York: Farrar, Straus and Giroux.

———. 1999. *Cat and Mouse in the Snow.* New York: Farrar, Straus and Giroux.

Bos, Burny. 2000. *Alexander the Great.* New York: North-South.

Buehner, Caralyn. 2004. *Superdog: The Heart of a Hero.* New York: HarperCollins.

Holm, Jennifer L., and Matthew Holm. 2005. *Babymouse: Our Hero.* New York: Random House.

O'Connor, George. 2005. *Ker-Splash!* New York: Simon & Schuster.

Pinkney, Brian. 1997. *The Adventures of Sparrow Boy.* New York: Simon & Schuster.

SanAngelo, Ryan. 2002. *Spaghetti Eddie.* Honesdale, Pa.: Boyds Mills Press.

References

Ashton-Warner, Sylvia. 1963. *Teacher.* New York: Simon & Schuster.

Baghban, Marcia. "Scribbles, Labels, and Stories: The Role of Drawing in the Development of Writing." *Young Children,* January 2007.

Bisson-Hohensee, Julie, and Louise Derman-Sparks. 1992. "Implementing an Anti-Bias Curriculum in Early Childhood." Clearinghouse on Early Education and Parenting. http://ceep.crc.uiuc.edu/eecearchive/digests/1992/hohens92.html.

Bowman, Barbara. "Standards at the Heart of Education Equity." NAEYC Beyond the Journal, September 2006. http://www.journal.naeyc.org/btj/200609/BowmanBTJ.asp.

Burns, M. Susan, Peg Griffin, and Catherine E. Snow, eds. 1999. *Starting Out Right: A Guide to Promoting Children's Reading Success.* Washington, D.C.: National Academy Press.

Codell, Esme Raji. Personal communication, June 4, 2006.

Cooper, Patsy. 1993. *When Stories Come to School: Telling, Writing, and Performing Stories in the Early Childhood Classroom.* New York: Teachers & Writers Collaborative.

Curenton, Stephanie M. "Oral Storytelling: A Cultural Art that Promotes School Readiness." *Young Children,* September 2006.

Curtis, Deb, and Margie Carter. 2000. *The Art of Awareness: How Observation Can Transform Your Teaching.* St. Paul, Minn.: Redleaf Press.

Derman-Sparks, Louise, and the A.B.C. Task Force. 1989. *Anti-Bias Curriculum: Tools for Empowering Young Children.* Washington, D.C.: National Association for the Education of Young Children.

Engel, Susan. 1999. *The Stories Children Tell: Making Sense of the Narratives of Childhood.* New York: W. H. Freeman.

Garbarino, James, and Frances M. Stott. 1992. *What Children Can Tell Us: Eliciting, Interpreting, and Evaluating Critical Information from Children.* San Francisco: Jossey-Bass.

Garvey, Catherine. 1977. *Play.* Cambridge, Mass.: Harvard University Press.

High/Scope Educational Research Foundation. "IEA Preprimary Project Age 7 Follow-up." High/Scope Educational Research Foundation. http://www.highscope.org/Research/International/iea_phase3summary.htm.

Jacobson, Linda. "Study Links Flexible Pre-K Classes to Skill Development." *Education Week,* September 9, 2006.

Joel, Peter, and Leslie Simonson. 1996. *Writing in Narrative: Story Writing by Dictation, A Three-Step Introduction.* Crossville, Tenn.: The Elijah Company.

Katch, Jane. 2001. *Under Deadman's Skin: Discovering the Meaning of Children's Violent Play.* Boston: Beacon Press.

Koplow, Leslie, ed. 1996. *Unsmiling Faces: How Preschools Can Heal.* New York: Teachers College Press.

Kreuger, Beverly S. "Charlotte Mason and Dictation." http://www.eclectichomeschool .org/articles/article.asp?articleid=423&resourceid=345.

Kusnetz, Ilyse. "Putting Her Life into Words." *Orlando Sentinel,* May 28, 2006.

Lester, Julius. "Kids Q & A." http://www.powells.com/kidsqa/lester.html (accessed June 13, 2007).

McLane, Joan Brooks, and Gillian Dowley McNamee. 1990. *Early Literacy.* Cambridge, Mass.: Harvard University Press.

McNamee, Gillian, Personal communication. July 14, 2006.

National Association for the Education of Young Children. "Many Languages, Many Cultures: Respecting and Responding to Diversity."Adapted from 1995 position statement of the National Association for the Education of Young Children. http://www.naeyc.org/about/positions/pdf/diversity.pdf.

———. "NAEYC Accreditation Criteria for Curriculum." http://www.naeyc.org/ academy/standards/standard2/standard2E.asp.

Neuman, Susan B., Carol Copple, and Sue Bredekamp. 2000. *Learning to Read and Write: Developmentally Appropriate Practices for Young Children.* Washington, D.C.: National Association for the Education of Young Children.

Paley, Vivian Gussin. "Storytelling and Story Acting with Vivian Paley." 1999. Muncie, Ind.: Ball State University. [Video]

———. "Storytelling Themes with Vivian Paley." 1999. Muncie, Ind.: Ball State University. [Video]

———. "Vivian Paley and the Boy Who Could Tell Stories." 1999. Muncie, Ind.: Ball State University. [Video]

———. 1997. *The Girl with the Brown Crayon.* Cambridge, Mass.: Harvard University Press.

———. 1990. *The Boy Who Would Be a Helicopter: The Uses of Storytelling in the Classroom.* Cambridge, Mass.: Harvard University Press.

———. 1984. *Boys and Girls: Superheroes in the Doll Corner.* Chicago: University of Chicago Press.

———. 1981. *Wally's Stories: Conversations in the Kindergarten.* Cambridge, Mass.: Harvard University Press.

Pardeck, John T., and Jean A. Pardeck, eds. 1993. *Bibliotherapy: A Clinical Approach for Helping Children.* Langhorne, Pa.: Gordon and Breach Science.